AF328919

GREAT
KIWI
FIRSTS

Astral is a travel writer and editor who now can spout random facts about the country she loves to anyone who cares to listen (now you have this book, you can too). Her first best-selling book, *Kiwi Toasties*, was the first New Zealand book to be shaped like a piece of toast.

www.greatkiwifirsts.com

# GREAT KIWI FIRSTS

ASTRAL SLIGO

ALLEN&UNWIN

SYDNEY · MELBOURNE · AUCKLAND · LONDON

First published in 2012

Copyright © Astral Sligo 2012

All rights reserved. No part of this book may be reproduced or transmitted in any form or by any means, electronic or mechanical, including photocopying, recording or by any information storage and retrieval system, without prior permission in writing from the publisher.

Allen & Unwin
Sydney, Melbourne, Auckland, London

Level 3, 228 Queen Street
Auckland 1010, New Zealand
Phone: (64 9) 377 3800

83 Alexander Street
Crows Nest NSW 2065, Australia
Phone: (61 2) 8425 0100
Email:  info@allenandunwin.com
Web:    www.allenandunwin.com

A catalogue record for this book is available from the National Library of New Zealand

ISBN 978 1 877505 22 5

Internal design by Brittany Britten
Index by Nicola McCloy
Cover photograph: Crowds greeting New Zealand aviatrix Jean Batten after she landed at Croydon, having flown from Australia, 24 October 1937.
Set in 10.75/14 pt Sabon LT Pro by Bookhouse, Sydney
Printed in Australia by Ligare Pty Ltd, Sydney

10 9 8 7 6 5 4 3 2 1

*Dedicated, with mucho aroha, to Mum, my foremost teacher and friend, and Dad, who showed me how to enjoy history.*

# CONTENTS

# INTRODUCTION

It is New Zealand's role to send out its bright young men
and women to help run the rest of the world. And they go,
not hating the country of their birth, but loving it. From
this loving base they make their mark on the world.

—Margaret Mead, American anthropologist

We are known for our pioneering spirit, for our ability to see beyond the strictures of what-hasn't-been-done-before, and New Zealand's intensely picturesque landscape is a backdrop for the mental landscape where ideas and fortitude flourish.

New Zealand's existence makes a difference, and within the pages of this non-linear social history book you'll find many examples of people who contributed to their community, country and the world.

Our landscape inspires us, our isolation pushes us to make our own way. The first people of New Zealand followed the stars to get here; in settling Aotearoa, the Maori people laid the foundations for our trailblazing Kiwi spirit. They were the first New Zealand agriculturalists, first horticulturalists, first to develop fortified citadels, first record-breaking sailors, first to search the skies and find knowledge from the stars, first to put their feet in the golden sands of an East Coast beach and first to negotiate the barrels of a West Coast beach.

In defending their land from incursions, they were innovators of trench warfare, accomplished and tactical warriors, yet in later years (Te Whiti at Parihaka) they showed the Europeans how to achieve strong and effective peaceful protest. Undoubtedly the Maori people notched up thousands of firsts as they crossed the seas in *waka*, explored forests for strong trees to provide shelter, and caught the first *kaimoana* platters to feed the first New Zealand families. So many firsts that are not told in written history. To a certain extent, the same can be said for many a first achieved by women, many of whose firsts have not been written down, or have been lost to time.

In selecting first stories to share, I admit to feeling that the reach of the book is vaster than one book alone. I find it difficult to imagine living anywhere other than New Zealand, where we were the first in so many arenas. First to give women the vote, first to really push for a nuclear-free status, first to see the sun (until Samoa changed its dateline), first to push the boundary between what is known and what is unknown in so many ways. Let's face it, we're pretty brilliant!

In my research, I found that history, despite what we may think, is endless. There are so many hidden nooks and crannies, so many stories to delve into, and vast seas of knowledge, whether curated or not, that can help bring the past to a clearer light. We're surrounded by it, but sometimes we just don't know where to look. Within the book I have tried to connect some of the firsts, and, where there are memorials or relics of the past, have mentioned these where possible, so that they may act as touchstones for the stories that you read here. Although it's impossible to have a first-hand experience of that first moment, it's nice to know when you can have a brush with a significant or intriguing part of our history.

We're a nation of contradictions. While we are keen to say 'don't fence me in', we are also quite good at fencing other things in and have been described by some as having a rather insular and parochial yet outward-looking society.

A few observations: many of the history makers within this book did not achieve their first because they were driven by the need to increase their fortune or popularity; they got there because they saw that there was a lack or a need for someone to do something, to provide answers for questions that may not have been verbalised. If you just go downstream all the time, and your thoughts always travel in the same direction, there is little likelihood that you will achieve a first.

Innovation seems to incubate (or fester, depending on your field) when your mind is not on the task—and a small spark of an idea, or a fully blown scheme may develop as you're paddling down a river in a bathtub, or running along pushing a milk-cart. Some firsts are accidental. Some are directed happenstance.

New events (firsts) in a lifetime are generally not created in the flash of some mad lightning-bolt moment of brilliance. It takes hours of effort, months of dedication, and sometimes years of just figuring it all out.

Kiwi ingenuity is the ability to spot the potential in the wide world, to put things together that don't normally go together, to take non-related disciplines and see what happens when they are forced into unanticipated collusion and collision. Everything builds on what has come before; although there is only a chance of doing one thing one way, there are many firsts that lead to a first. By utilising existing pieces of knowledge, skill and insight and using our personal energy, time and talent we shape new firsts.

The personality-profile of us as a nation is one characterised by self-reliance, innovation and, perhaps our Achilles heel, reticence. Whether it be for fear of being accused of being a tall poppy, or the genuine wish to 'not make a fuss', we can sometimes keep our problems and our triumphs to ourselves, which means we may miss out on an opportunity to share a problem, and to proclaim a first. A problem shared may be a problem halved, but a first success is a first amplified. Sometimes we may fear being thought of as the oddball, the strange person who retreats to the back shed and tinkers away because we believe that there is a better, quicker way of doing something. Really, what may be thought of as delusional behaviour, should be reclassified as a vision of the future.

Expose your idea to the light of day and see if it sticks together in the glare of that crisp New Zealand light.

It's great that Australia (2012 population: 22,880,619) has invented the dual-flush toilet, and Chateau cardboard (wine in a cardboard cask) among other things, but with a population of 4,432,620 New Zealand's impact on the world is nothing short of back-slapping, blow-me-down-you-little-beauty brilliant.

Let's aim for many more Great Kiwi Firsts!

# 1

# TOUCHING THE SKIES

## FLYING BOAT

*First to take off from the sea*

Who said Kiwis can't fly—or float, for that matter? On 1 January 1915 the first flying boat flight in New Zealand took off from the Waitemata harbour, Auckland. Engineer and engine importer Vivian Walsh and his brother Leo had designed and built what was probably the first flying boat in the southern hemisphere.

Prior to that, in 1909, they had constructed their first aeroplane from imported kitsets, which Vivian taught himself to fly with absolutely no instructions. (The brothers were later the Boeing Company's first ever customers, buying in kitset form the first Boeing plane sold in the world.) Along with a few other enthusiasts, fascinated by accounts of aviation adventures in the northern hemisphere, they formed the Aero Club of

The biplane 'Manurewa', built by the Walsh brothers.
The man in the pilot's seat is probably Vivian Walsh

New Zealand in 1910 and helped to lay the foundations for both military and civil aviation in New Zealand. In March 1915, Vivian took the first of many passengers on a flight of five miles.

The brothers later set up a flying school with a base at Mission Bay, Auckland, to train air pilots for the First World War when flying boats were operated by the Royal Flying Corps (later the Royal New Zealand Air Force) to keep the far-flung island outposts of the British Empire connected. The first pilot's certificate was issued to Vivian Walsh on 13 July 1916 (you can see it at the Museum of Transport and Technology (MOTAT)).

By the end of 1918, 110 pilots had been trained and posted. After the war the school continued and the superbly trained ex-military pilots gave civilian aviation a boost.

After many months of Leo trying to convince the government of the functional value of air transport, on 16 December 1919 the first official airmail flight within New Zealand took place between Auckland and Dargaville. Just over a year later, New Zealand's first regular airmail service began with the Canterbury Aviation Company's delivery from the western outskirts of Christchurch, bound for Ashburton and Timaru.

In 1938, 25,000 letters, parcels and postcards were carried on the first official New Zealand airmail run (see first airmail stamps page 265) to the United States. The Pan American flying boat took off from Mechanics Bay in Auckland on 2 January, had a stopover and cargo transferral in Honolulu, and carried on to San Francisco, arriving there on 6 January.

During the war, the Kiwi pilots trained at the Walsh's school had mastered the art of aeronautical island-hopping and putting down lightly on the turquoise waters of tropical lagoons. What was intended to be simply a scheduled flying-boat mail service, linking South Seas islands scattered over thousands of miles, soon became the most romantic airline route in the world, known as the Coral Route. TEAL introduced the service in 1951, ferrying passengers from Auckland's harbour across to Fiji, Samoa, Tahiti and the Cook Islands in luxurious two-deck Solent IV flying boats.

Carrying about 45 passengers, the aircraft had silver service, tables with linen tablecloths, an on-board chef, and powder rooms. Passengers dressed in their finery were advised to carry bathing suits in their hand luggage so they could take a dip in a lagoon while the plane refuelled.

The last Coral Route service (and the last commercial flying boat service in the world) had its final landing at Mechanics Bay on 14 September 1960. The only remaining Solent IV in the world is on display at the MOTAT aircraft hangar in Auckland where it has been restored by members of the original flight crew and enthusiasts from the Solent Preservation Society.

There is a statue at Auckland's Mission Bay to commemorate both Walsh brothers.

# RICHARD PEARSE 1877–1953

*First heavier than air powered flight*

If you achieve a world first at anything it may pay to shout the fact from the rooftops—or hedgetops in this case—rather than skim them.

Richard Pearse was more likely to discuss his golf handicap or enthuse about tennis than tell you that he made and flew the first heavier than air, powered flying machine.

At a time when the prevailing thought was guided by the conservative view that if men were supposed to fly they would have wings, Pearse, who was not born with wings, had the brains and the drive to create them. But the outright ingenuity of this quiet and reclusive South Canterbury man was not recognised until after his death.

The son of Digory Pearse and Sarah Browne, Richard was the fourth child of nine. The Pearse family was as abundant in talent as it was in members; they all excelled at chess and tennis, and formed their own small orchestra with Richard playing the cello.

Home life on the large farm in rugged Waitohi, South Canterbury, seems to have been perfectly suited to such a rambling and clever bunch. The Pearse family kept company with an eclectic and eccentric assortment of pets including goats, guinea pigs, ferrets, rabbits (Canterbury farmers now know who to partly blame for today's epidemic), dogs and parading pheasants and peacocks, a parrot who served as the call for breakfast, and a pet monkey who wore a hat and sucked on a smoking pipe. It seems like a storybook environment for an inventive genius to grow up in.

As a schoolboy, Richard was said to be a bit of a dreamer, a bit of a bookworm and every bit driven to study engineering. One of his first inventions was a mechanical needle-threading device—a gift for his mother. Unfortunately, his father could not afford to send him to university, so when Richard left school at sixteen, he went to work on the family farm.

In 1898, on his twenty-first birthday, Richard was given a 100-acre block of the family's land to farm for himself, but his heart wasn't in it. His younger brother recalled that it was not unusual to see Richard trailing behind his plough horses with his head in a book or an engineering magazine.

He turned the old cottage on the land into a workshop with a forge and a lathe (which he built from parts largely found at the local tip), and began building his own inventions; it seems he was working on ideas for powered flight from this time on.

The industrious and innovative Pearse still lived at his parents' farm, cycling to his workshop and increasingly run-down farm, often working long into the night on his contraptions. Appropriately, the first invention that he sought a patent for was a bamboo-framed bicycle where the pedals were pushed up and down, rather than around, and had integrated tyre pumps which allowed a flat tyre to be tended to while still riding.

One evening in 1902, an almighty racket that frightened sheep, cattle and the sleeping potato farmers of the peaceable Waitohi area heralded the life-spark of Pearse's first lightweight 2-cylinder 25-horsepower petrol engine. To achieve flight, it was necessary to make an engine significantly smaller than the car engines of the time; Pearse, probably with some advice from petrolhead Cecil Wood (see page 44), accomplished this, his engine weighing in at only 57 kilograms.

It was then a matter of a few months and many, many hours of dedicated dabbling before Pearse would move from rambling around the paddock with his noisy 'beast' (as one neighbour put it) to making his first public attempts at flight.

He'd been busy constructing an aircraft to go with the engine. The mono-wing had a tricycle undercarriage and was constructed of bamboo, wire, canvas and bits of tubular steel Pearse had adapted and crafted with his own forge and lathe. Even the pistons were made from tinkered with tobacco tins; Pearse put the craft into aircraft.

After putting the engine into the aircraft, he tested the control and thrust. Then one day, watched by a small gathering of locals, Pearse taxied down the Main Waitohi Road and achieved enough sustained lift to have the aircraft pitch into one of the immense 3-metre high gorse hedges surrounding his property (clearly, he had higher things to consider than controlling gorse). Although there are no official records of this event and the eyewitness accounts were only gathered years later, it is thought that the craft was in the air for a distance of at least 50 metres (possibly up to a couple of hundred) on 31 March 1903—seven and a half months before the Wright brothers' flight.

Witnesses said that after the plane's engine was started (Richard's younger brother Warne pulled the propeller) and the boulders holding back the machine were pushed away, Pearse accelerated and the craft slowly climbed into the air but pitched and wobbled about, moving at about 30 kilometres per hour. It then veered to the left and crashed into the top of the gorse hedge, turfing Pearse out and leaving him with an injured shoulder. But he had flown the world's first powered take-off!

To put things in perspective, even on 17 December 1903, when Wilbur and Orville Wright claim to have made the first flight, they only achieved this with the help of a 60-foot launching (mono)rail which their plane rode down a small incline atop a wheeled dolly. Their first recorded flight was 120 feet (36.5 metres) and lasted all of 12 seconds. The Wright's first flight at Kitty Hawk was witnessed and captured by a photographer; a Temuka photographer had taken a few snaps of Pearse's hedge-locked plane the day after the first New Zealand flight, but a subsequent flood ruined his entire portfolio.

Pearse persevered with his attempts to fly and in 1906 applied to patent his aircraft design—including the world's first examples of moveable wing flaps, the world's first aileron controls (variable lift).

In the 1930s, Richard started work on his second aircraft, the Utility Craft. Pearse believed it would be so cheap to produce and handy to use that every family would have one in their backyard. This more powerful aircraft had an engine that could be tilted from the vertical to the horizontal—basically transforming it from an airplane into a helicopter capable of vertical take-off and landing, and eliminating the need for a runway. If Pearse's machine had been taken up by the aircraft companies he tried to get interest from (decades later, the Harrier 'jump jet' was invented in Britain), we may have currently thought nothing of taking a quick flight to get the groceries, or pick up the kids from school and, with fold-away wings, parking it in the garage afterwards.

Unfortunately, lacking the engineering education to truly finesse his ideas as well the financial backers, and encountering bureaucratic bumbling in his patent applications, our great inventor developed a disillusionment with the world and started to believe that people were out to steal his inventions. After a lifetime of ridicule from those unable to set their eyes above the horizon, Richard Pearse was admitted to Sunnyside Mental Hospital in 1951; two years later he suffered a heart attack and died at the age of 75.

In the days before Supercheap Auto and Mitre10 Mega, Pearse was the epitome of our inventive bloke banished by self-exile to an isolated shed in the back paddock.

Pearse's achievement is even more remarkable when you start to break down the facts.

He had no formal engineering training but the intricate and detailed technical drawings of his inventions show an acute mind with an enviable amount of prescience.

It was unlikely that he would have even laid eyes on a manufactured petrol-powered engine, although he did keep up with the Joneses (or, rather ahead of the Wrights) by reading *Scientific American*.

Whereas the Wright brothers in America had a team of engineers at their disposal, and later were granted government funding to pursue their flying fixation, Pearse was a one-man production unit and thought of as an oddball rather than an innovator.

Pearse's birthday—3 December—should be a national holiday to celebrate Kiwi ingenuity, where we all head to the shed and make something—anything. Who knows, it may just be the first ever something-or-other (though possibly most of the country would actually use this day to get the Christmas shopping done).

# JEAN BATTEN 1909–82

*First to make a direct flight between England and New Zealand*

Every flyer who ventures across oceans to distant lands is a potential explorer; in his or her breast burns the same fire that urged adventurers of old to set forth in their sailing ships for foreign lands.

—Jean Batten, *Alone In The Sky*

In October 1937, ten thousand people gathered at London's Croydon airport to greet a young female pilot who had just smashed the Australia–England solo record, making her an aviation legend.

The Garbo of the Skies, a beautiful girl with dark hair and a white flying suit, Jean Batten was hailed as one of the best women pilots of the twentieth century.

Despite enormous adulation, Kiwi flying first Jean hung up her goggles in 1939, and entered into a life of seclusion for more than forty years. Her disappearance into a lonely private life came to public attention in the 1980s when her publisher hadn't heard from her for many years and investigations into her whereabouts led to the discovery

The Garbo of the Skies/Hine-o-te-Rangi/Jean Batten—the beautiful
girl in the flying machine (seen here at Rongotai airport, Wellington)
was no plain Jane

that Jean had died in bizarre and tragic circumstances in a seedy suburb
on the Spanish island of Majorca in 1982. She had been bitten by a
dog and, refusing to seek medical help, she had died in her apartment
from a pulmonary infection—the wound had become septic, spreading
infection to her lungs—and, without any family contacts, she had been
buried in a pauper's grave.

Born in 1909 in Rotorua to a dentist father and an actress mother,
Jane Gardner Batten, known as Jean, would become New Zealand's most

famous daughter in the 1930s. (Perhaps if the daring and determined Jean had grown up to be a plain Jane, then she may not have achieved all she did.) From the cradle, Jean was destined to fly—her mother pinned a newspaper clipping of the Wright brothers' flight on baby Jean's bassinet.

When she was four, the family moved to Auckland, and on weekend strolls Jean would be taken to watch the seaplanes take off from Kohimarama beach (see Walsh brothers, page 1). It was here that she first became aware of an urge to be up among the clouds.

When she was fifteen, Jean enrolled in a secretarial course, and also donned ballet shoes and practised her piano scales, hoping to become a professional performer.

However, her mother—a woman of strong ideas who instilled in Jean the belief that to survive in a man's world, you had to excel at male pursuits—had other ideas and actively encouraged Jean's aviation obsession. On a holiday to Sydney she even arranged for Jean to take her first-ever flight with Australian flying hero Sir Charles Kingsford Smith, who was the first person to fly across the Tasman. Jean flew over the Blue Mountains in his plane, the *Southern Cross*, in 1930. In the air, Jean felt completely at home, later saying, 'Cruising about high above the Blue Mountains I had felt completely at home in the air and decided that here indeed was my element.'

While Jean's father vehemently disagreed with the prospect of his daughter flying planes, he was at odds with Jean's mother who helped Jean sell her piano to buy an airfare to England and colluded further so the two of them left New Zealand for England—leaving Jean's father and brothers behind.

Arriving in England in 1930, Jean wasted no time becoming the first New Zealand female to secure the British Air Ministry's A licence by learning to fly at the London Aeroplane Club. With just twenty hours clocked in the skies, Jean began to plan a solo flight from England to Australia, determined to break the women's record of nineteen and a half days, set earlier that year by the English pilot Amy Johnson. She ensured that her preparation for this solo endeavour included learning navigation, and studying weather patterns and engine maintenance.

In April 1933, Jean set off from England in what proved to be a frightening yet ultimately failed attempt at flying to Australia. Caught by numerous sandstorms over Iraq, and suffering engine failure over Karachi, Jean miraculously escaped a crash landing unharmed, but her aircraft was wrecked.

A year later the resolute Kiwi aviatrix set off again. This time, zig-zagging between a maze of radio masts in Italy and running out of fuel, she skilfully crash-landed the Gipsy Moth plane in the dark. She had the plane returned to England, had it repaired and then two days later made her third attempt, leaving England on 8 May 1934.

Fourteen days and 22 and a half hours later, Jean Batten arrived in Darwin, shattering Johnson's record by over four days and winning world celebrity and the adulation of her nation overnight. She then proceeded to make a six-week tour of her homeland, attending banquets and parades in her honour.

On 11 November 1935, Jean set out from London in a brilliant navigational accomplishment, flying from England to South America and with only a watch and compass to guide her, made the 3057 kilometre leg over the treacherous South Atlantic to Port Natal, Brazil. Batten completed the transatlantic trip in 13 hours, 15 minutes from West Africa to Brazil. She established another world record for being the first woman to fly solo across the South Atlantic.

A year later Jean broke all records—both male and female—flying the 22,530 kilometres from England to New Zealand, crossing, in a dangerous feat, the treacherous Tasman Sea. Because she was travelling in the opposite direction to the sun, Jean would lose two hours of daylight on her journey, so her navigation calculations had to be accurate; without a radio, life raft, or modern-day tracking systems, she faced death. The solo flight from England to New Zealand had taken eleven days and 40 minutes, a record which Jean held for more than 40 years.

Her arrival at Auckland airport caused a 20-kilometre long traffic jam as 6000 Kiwis rushed to welcome their aviation heroine. Auckland Mayor Ernest Davis greeted her with a congratulatory speech that still managed to be condescending:

Jean you are a very naughty girl, and really I think you want a good spanking for giving us such a terribly anxious time here. We knew you could do it, but

we did not want you to run the risk. We glory in what you have done, and
we glory in your wonderful and magnificent pluck, dear. We congratulate
you from the bottom of our hearts.

She toured the country, and returning to her birthplace of Rotorua she
was honoured by local Maori, given the title Hine-o-te-Rangi—'Daughter
of the Skies'—and gifted a chief's feather cloak.

In 1937, at the age of 28, Jean Batten made her last long-distance
flight—this time flying from New Zealand via Australia to England in
five days and eighteen hours. This feat established a solo record (for pilots
of either sex), and Jean became the first person to simultaneously hold
England–Australia solo flight records in both directions. Although her
head may have been in the clouds, her heart was touched by the sight of
the ten-thousand strong crowd who had gathered to watch this occasion.

When I flew over Croydon the most amazing sight met my eyes. The
boundaries of the aerodrome were black with people and a huge crowd
had assembled to greet me. As I glided down to a landing, then taxied up
to the tarmac, I felt deeply moved.

During the Second World War the plane that she had flown across the
world was commissioned into active service for Britain, and Jean was
unable to fly it.

Jean was created Commander of the British Empire (CBE) in 1936,
and she was given the Cross of Chevalier of the French Legion of Honour

the same year. In 1938, she was awarded the medal of the Fédération Aéronautique Internationale, aviation's highest honour, the first woman to receive it. Jean wrote about her adventures in two autobiographies.

Despite being known for her pretty face and her fierce determination and gumption, Jean Batten was a complex character whose glamorous life—she would often disembark wearing make-up and ready to attend whatever fête was put on for her—belied the loneliness that she felt. Many men felt attracted to this 'mere girl' while others felt challenged by her independence—an Otago Harbour Board once rejected the possibility of awarding her 50 guineas because they didn't want to encourage other women to aim for such unwomanly things as flying planes.

By 1946, Jean had mostly left the public eye and joined her mother living in Jamaica. In the 1950s they both went on an extended gypsy-like roadtrip lasting seven years. Although Jean's mother could be seen to be the driving force behind her daughter's ruthless yet glamorous determination, it has been suggested that such an intense relationship also drove Jean away from the society that so adored her. When her mother died, Jean was devastated and moved to Tenerife where she lived for sixteen years before eventually moving to Majorca.

Six years after Jean's death, the then Minister of Women's Affairs, Margaret Shields, unveiled a bronze plaque with a sculpted image of Batten and commemorative text in Spanish and English on the site of Jean Batten's grave in Majorca. A nearby street was also renamed Carrer de Jean Batten.

Streets in Auckland, Christchurch, Mount Maunganui, Wellington and Rotorua are named after this Kiwi pioneer, and—although you very rarely hear it—the international terminal at Auckland airport is officially the Jean Batten International Terminal—look for her Gull monoplane that hangs above the terminal's duty free centre. And wave at the statue of Batten outside the airport. In Mangere, South Auckland, the Jean Batten Primary School holds a speech and music competition from a fund left to it by Batten—it was the school that honoured her landing in 1936.

Jean Batten's life broke the barriers of history, flight, distance, gender roles (see John Money, page 120) and adventure—she is a great Kiwi first.

# THE MARTIN JETPACK

*The world's first practical jetpack*

At the Experimental Aircraft Association's 2008 gathering in Wisconsin, Kiwi Glenn Martin unveiled a prototype for the world's first practical jetpack, capable of flying at speeds of up to 100 kilometres per hour at an altitude of 8000 feet for half an hour on a full tank. Previous jetpacks have only been able to fly for perhaps a minute of air time, so this sustained flight is a first.

The Martin jetpack uses a premium gasoline engine with two ducted fans providing sufficient thrust to lift the aircraft and a pilot in vertical take-off and landing. The jetpack is a practical flying vehicle initially developed for the leisure market, but perhaps realising that a casual user may find the outlay and upkeep of a $75,000 pleasure craft a tad prohibitive, the team at Martin Aircraft Company in Christchurch promote their jetpack to the military, civil defence and entertainment recreation (i.e. stadium shows) sectors. It is easy to see how a jetpack would be particularly useful for search and rescue.

Glenn Martin's invention wasn't an overnight success, the development of the pack came after 27 years of research and development.

## PETER LYNN 1946–

*First to make giant octopuses fly*

If you've ever looked to the skies and been awed by a giant inflatable kite in the shape of an animal or sea creature, chances are you were admiring Peter Lynn's work. Peter is the engineer turned kitemaker who has been at the forefront of pioneering kite design. In 1973 he made his first kite and within a decade was exporting his designs all around the world. He now spends much of his time exhibiting at international kite fairs, earning himself the nickname of 'roving kite ambassador'.

Rather than using a fixed rib to strengthen the interior of a kite, Peter was the first to employ adjustable yet super-strong nylon cords for the interior framework of the kite.

His successful kite export business allowed him to spend time writing scientific papers on the theoretical aspects of kite flying, and researching and developing the concept of kite traction in the form of sand buggies, kite-sailing and kite-surfing equipment.

The sport of kite buggying in its modern form began with a kite-sailing craft Peter worked on in the late 1980s. Adapting power kites for traction use, the buggies harness the wind to pull adventurers along at high speeds, and he built boats, buggies, boards and snow sleds to use with them. The concept of a kite buggy is not a new idea; they were known in thirteenth-century China and a British inventor in 1827 also promoted the idea. Buggies were commercially available in the late 1970s but it took Peter Lynn's creativity and aerodynamic expertise to introduce strong, lightweight, affordable three-wheeled buggies in the early 1990s, which then led to the popularisation of the sport and hobby. Ashburton's Argyle Park was his testing ground with kite buggies reaching speeds of up to 100 kilometres per hour. His pioneering designs are now recognised and 10,000 of his buggies are zooming around the world.

He was the first to design and patent the arc kite or twin-skin kite—a type of traction power kite suitable for pulling small crafts or vehicles and people along at high speeds, but agile enough to allow an adventurer some control. You'll see them in action when kite surfers skim across the water.

In 1995, Peter attained his first Guinness world record by designing the world's largest kite at 635 square metres, which could host more than 1000 people comfortably mingling inside it, when on the ground. His second entry in the book is for the current Guinness record of the largest kite, made from a 1019 square metre Kuwaiti flag. Perhaps soon he will make a Kiwi flag that beats even that.

When not flying kites, Peter also manages the Lynn Historical Woodworking Museum in Ashburton where the world's number one collection of nineteenth century ornamental turning lathes resides. It's a collection his father devoted his life to, and is highly regarded among international woodturning enthusiasts.

**2**

# THROUGH THE LOOKING GLASS TO INFINITY AND BEYOND

## SIR WILLIAM HAYWARD PICKERING 1910–2004

*First Kiwi to lead space exploration*

In the mid-1950s, Russia and America were working on sending satellites to the edge of Earth's atmosphere, the beginnings of space exploration. It was a race, and not the most friendly of races, so the Americans were rather upset when Russia's satellite *Sputnik* was launched in 1957. Circling Earth every 90 minutes, *Sputnik*'s transmitter beeped and every beep—which could be heard from any shortwave radio on Earth—reminded the Americans that a Russian craft was flying above American skies and invading their space.

The American Navy had been charged with sending up a test rocket satellite, but the big budget *Vanguard* exploded upon launch in December

1957 with the international media watching. Faces were red and egos were bruised.

Luckily, a Kiwi was on the job. William Pickering, who was born in Wellington on Christmas Eve 1910 and had attended the same primary school as Ernest Rutherford (see page 121), was the director at the Jet Propulsion Laboratory (JPL) in Pasadena, California, which was trying to find a satellite delivery system on a smaller budget than the navy.

*Explorer 1* was successfully launched from Cape Canaveral, Florida, on 31 January 1958, less than four months after *Sputnik*. It orbited the Earth for the next ten years.

In 1958 the National Aeronautics and Space Administration (NASA) was established and JPL was transferred to NASA. It was a dream job for the man who had been encouraged by his science and maths teacher, Charles Gifford (see page 30) to have his first look through a telescope at the Wellington College Observatory. Of his JPL job, Pickering said, 'I had a charter that basically said "go out and explore the solar system".'

He'd attended Canterbury University College but completed his bachelor's degree at the California Institute of Technology (Caltech) and later a PhD in physics in 1936.

William had thought in the 1930s that he'd return to New Zealand to work in the developing electrical power business but jobs were scarce so he accepted a teaching position at Caltech. And from there took the JPL job. 'I had no thought that this position would develop into space

William H. Pickering, (centre) director of NASA's Jet Propulsion Laboratory, presents a model of the Mariner spacecraft to President John F. Kennedy in 1961. (NASA)

projects. At that time no-one except a few wild-eyed science fiction fans had any idea that space exploration would happen,' he said.

William Pickering led America's unmanned deep space research. Under his 22-year directorship at JPL, the first close-up high-resolution pictures of the Moon were taken by the Ranger missions, the *Surveyor* craft made lunar landings, and space craft were sent to Mercury, Venus and Mars (see Zorbing page 155). Pickering is the first Kiwi to have his name in space when his digitised signature travelled to Mars on board one of the Rover modules.

He became known as 'Mr JPL' and was featured twice on the cover of *Time* magazine. In 2002 he returned to New Zealand to be awarded an honorary doctorate by the University of Canterbury, two years before his death. Although he was made an American citizen in 1941, he never forgot his homeland, and he established the WH Pickering Fellowship for New Zealand graduates to study engineering or science at Caltech. Thomas Everhart, the president of Caltech, said of Pickering: 'More than any other individual, Bill Pickering was responsible for America's success in exploring the planets—an endeavour that demanded vision, courage, dedication, expertise and the ability to inspire two generations of scientists and engineers'. And NASA administrator, Dr Ed Weiler, also had high praise: 'Dr Pickering brought a vision and passion to space exploration that was remarkable. His pioneering work is the very foundation we have built upon to explore our solar system and beyond'.

In 2009 to mark the International Year of Astronomy, William Hayward Pickering was selected along with cosmologist Beatrice Tinsley (see page 35) to have their names bestowed on peaks in the Kepler mountains of Fiordland National Park. In Auckland's industrial suburb of Albany there is William Pickering Drive, but to top that, in December 2010, the New Zealand Geographic Board gazetted Mount Pickering as an official New Zealand place name.

# ANDREW CAMERON 1958–

*First to see a planet orbit in the opposite direction to its host star*

Andrew Collier Cameron is a Kiwi expatriate and expert planet hunter who, as a professor of astronomy in the School of Physics and Astronomy at the University of St Andrews, Scotland, led a team of British scientists in the quest to discover planets in other solar systems by looking for the dips in light that occur when planets pass between us and their host stars.

Among their discoveries are a number of firsts. These include WASP-17b, the first planet found to orbit in the direction opposite to its host star's spin. The discovery of this large planet in the constellation Scorpius changed traditional planetary theory and the understanding of the way planetary systems can rearrange themselves through violent gravitational interactions between planets.

Andrew's team also found WASP-18b, the first known planet that orbits so close to its star that tidal forces will cause it to plunge into its star within the next few million years. WASP-18b is approximately 3.1 million kilometres from its star, which is about 325 light years from Earth. One light year is just under 10 trillion kilometres. He first developed an interest in astronomy as a kid growing up under spectacularly dark skies in rural Nelson, and eventually pursued it via a physics degree followed by a PhD in astronomy at the University of Canterbury. Andrew continues to scope the skies for signs of out-of-this-world worlds.

# ROY KERR—COSMIC TITAN 1934-

*First to solve one of Einstein's equations about general relativity*

Not only was Roy Kerr the first to solve one of Einstein's equations about general relativity, but he was the discoverer of rotating black holes—the theoretical discovery that is the basis for almost all research in astrophysics today.

Fans of sci-fi TV series and films will be all too familiar with the vague and looming power of a rogue rotating black hole and the effect this may have on a spaceship trying to boldly make it through deep space where none have gone before. Or perhaps you've discussed the concept of using such black holes as a one-way wormhole for adventurous travel to the future or past, and even as a possible gateway to a parallel universe.

Black holes are now an accepted part of our unknown and known cosmos, but for many years eminent scientists thought that black holes—or dark stars as they were previously called—were rather preposterous; even Albert Einstein had declared that they 'do not exist in physical reality', but could—in true science ways—exist in theory.

In 1915, Einstein did as he did best and came up with field equations of general relativity (how gravitation is created by the geometry of space–time and the masses and vacuums present—I think!) that had no known solutions.

Numerous scientists tried to solve this riddle, many saying it could not be done, and some coming close, but only creating solutions that catered to one specific part of Einstein's highly non-linear equation. In 1916, Karl Schwarzschild came up with an answer for static black holes, but it became evident that just as stars and planets rotate, it was most likely that black holes did too.

Then, in 1963, Roy Kerr, a 29-year-old from Kurow, north west of Oamaru, announced his solution to this incredibly complex problem, since described as 'the most important exact solution to any equation in physics'.

Kerr had started his academic career at the University of Canterbury in 1951, where in his first year he had taken third-year mathematics papers and sat in on master's lectures. Although obviously bright, Roy wasn't a regular cardie-wearing boffin; he was a self-confessed party animal, spending a great deal of time playing billiards and alarming his lecturers by representing his college as a light-welterweight boxer.

With his brain thankfully undamaged by boxing, Kerr attained his MSc with first-class honours, was granted a scholarship and headed off to Cambridge where he was awarded a PhD. America was his next destination, where he was employed by the Aeronautical Research Laboratory in Dayton, Ohio, but not—as was rumoured—to develop an anti-gravity engine to power spaceships. Moving to the University of Texas in 1962, he was assimilated into a group of people thinking about relativity.

In a characteristically Kiwi way, Roy shares an insight into how important science gets done:

Everybody who tried to solve the problem was going at it from the front, but I was trying to solve the equation from a different point of view—there were a number of new mathematical methods coming into relativity at the time . . . I was trying to look at the whole structure . . . and it all seemed to be pretty nice and it looked like lots of solutions were going to come out. Then I hit a brick wall.

Teddy Newman and Roger Penrose were working on a similar set of methods, but Teddy had come out with this as-yet unpublished theorem that basically 'proved' that my solution couldn't exist! Luckily, my neighbour, who was playing around with relativity, too, got hold of a preprint and I just scanned through it (I'm a lazy reader) and hit the crucial part which proved to me that my solution could exist! After that, I kept working like mad and found the solution in a few weeks.

Kerr's solution, using the equation that is now known as the Kerr metric, correctly and elegantly described how space–time behaves in the four-dimensional world around supermassive objects such as steadily rotating stars or black holes. Such black holes are described only by their mass and angular momentum. Kerr showed that there is a vortex-like region outside the maw of the hole that drags space and time around with the rotating hole.

It was a revolution in astrophysics, but like many revolutions, the groundswell support and recognition didn't come until later. When recognition came, it was emphatic (although mostly from people outside New Zealand).

With terms such as 'orthonormal components of the Riemann tensor', 'affinely parameterised timelike geodesic' and the intriguing 'killing vectors' being part and parcel of the Kerr metric, it's little wonder that most of us can't quite appreciate the true significance of Roy Kerr's thinking. But Kerr is lauded as one of the greatest ever mathematicians and scientists of our time, admired by the likes of Stephen Hawking and virtually swooned over by legendary astrophysicist S. Chandrasekhar, who nominated Kerr for a Nobel Prize, and said of him in a 1975 lecture at the University of Chicago:

> In my entire scientific life, extending over forty-five years, the most shattering experience has been the realization that an exact solution of Einstein's equations of general relativity, discovered by the New Zealand mathematician, Roy Kerr, provides the absolutely exact representation of untold numbers of massive black holes that populate the universe. This shuddering before the beautiful, this incredible fact that a discovery motivated by a search after the beautiful in mathematics should find its exact replica in Nature, persuades me to say that beauty is that to which the human mind responds at its deepest and most profound.

Stephen Hawking used Kerr's accomplishment to refine and expand on modern astronomy and physics. Nowadays it is believed that more than 300 million supermassive black holes are at the heart of galaxies across the cosmos.

Returning to New Zealand in 1971, where he took up the post of lecturer and then head of the mathematics department at his former university, Kerr represented the country at championship level bridge, drove American sportscars and continued to be a revolutionary thinker. Perhaps one of the greatest minds of the twentieth century, Roy Kerr retired in 1993, and in 2004 a 'Kerrfest' was held at the University of Canterbury to celebrate Roy's seventieth birthday—bringing 50 top international scientists to Christchurch to honour this Kiwi.

Among the many awards recognising Roy Kerr's contributions are the Hughes Medal (1984) from the Royal Society, the Hector Medal (1982), the Rutherford Medal (1993) from the Royal Society of New Zealand, and the prestigious Marcel Grossman Award in 2006. His relativism colleague Professor Fulvio Melia wrote a book in 2009 titled *Cracking the Einstein Code*, which is essentially a biography of Roy. In the 2011 New Year's Honours list, Roy Kerr was given the award of Companion of the New Zealand Order of Merit (CNZM) for his services to astrophysics.

The man is a legend, and should be known to as many people in his home country as outside it.

# ALGERNON CHARLES GIFFORD 1862–1948

*First to state the reason for the Moon's crater face*

In 1924 and 1930, Charles Gifford, a mathematics teacher at Wellington College, contested the view that the Moon's craters were volcanic in origin, and provided mathematical equations demonstrating that these lunar depressions were formed by the impact of meteorites. Unfortunately, Gifford died before his theory was proved to be correct when space missions reached the Moon decades later.

Gifford was born on the *Zealandia* off the coast of the Cape of Good Hope while his family were en route to settle in Oamaru from England. He was a gifted Kiwi amateur astronomer who in 1912 established an educational observatory to encourage a new generation of stargazers. The observatory had an impressive 130-millimetre refractor telescope and is located on Mount Victoria in the grounds of Wellington College.

After several decades of disrepair, the Gifford Memorial Observatory was repaired and maintained in 2000, ready for use primarily by school groups and the Wellington Astronomical Society. A mural on its exterior depicts William Pickering, who officially opened the 'second light' (see Pickering, page 21) of the observatory in March 2002, and another mural at the entrance of the observatory depicts 'Uncle Charlie'.

Charles Gifford was also an explorer and one of the early photographic documenters of the South Island's back country.

Gifford was to New Zealand astronomy what meteors were to the moon: a face-changing impact

# ALBERT FRANCIS ARTHUR LOFLEY JONES 1920–

*The first 80-year-old (and oldest person ever) to discover a comet*

*The first to witness the death throes (and thus first
appearance of) the famous Supernova 1987A*

Amateur astronomer Albert Jones, a retired shopkeeper living in Nelson, is proof that there is always more to life than what first meets the eye. Even as an 80-year-old, Albert Jones had keen observational skills that were sharper than those of many youngsters—a trait that has led some astronomers to state that he has calibrated eyeballs.

Born in Christchurch on 9 August 1920, educated in Linwood and later in Timaru, Albert made his first telescope in the late 1930s from a paper tube, created by papier-mâchéing around the hose of the family's vacuum cleaner (in those days there were few cardboard tubes), and a couple of lenses. Although very crude, it still enabled him to observe the Orion nebula.

He attained his university entrance, but at the time, during the Great Depression, he decided that getting a job was less likely to interfere with his astronomic variable observations than furthering his education would.

Albert taught himself the location of stars and the night-sky map in order to satisfy his curiosity—never thinking he would make a stellar contribution to the world's astronomical knowledge base.

He wanted to see more than just the Moon and planets, and his imagination was piqued by the aurora which was visible from the family bach on the banks of the Rakaia River. It was here that he observed and made notes on a brilliant aurora, sending them off to the Carter Observatory in Wellington. They responded favourably to his observations and kept him updated with all things astronomical, including nominating him to be a member of the first New Zealand Astronomical Society.

He spotted his first comet in 1946—comet Jones 1946 h—and in 2001 discovered his second comet—c2000 W1—giving him the record of the longest period between comet discoveries, a gap of 54 years.

The night he discovered the brightest extra-galactic supernova in history, he had been at a hiking club meeting and had declined to stay on for the social chit-chat in order to get to his telescope and observe the southern skies. (Albert met his wife at the tramping club—finding his soulmate, it is joked, is his best discovery.) It was 24 February 1987 and the high summer skies got dark at 10 p.m. Noticing cloud cover approaching, Albert decided to quickly check on some stars in the Large Magellanic Cloud before they were obscured, and using his homemade 12-inch telescope, built in 1948, he found an unexpected bright blue star. As clouds covered the view, he phoned in his discovery of this 'bright stranger' to colleague and mentor Frank Bateson, director of the Variable Star section of the Royal Astronomical Society of New Zealand.

What was later stated to be the brightest explosion of a dying star to be seen with the naked eye since the seventeenth century, the supernova was photographed in 1994 by the Hubble space telescope. The explosion took place about 170,000 years ago, and Albert Jones was the first to see and record this explosion.

Professional astronomers from around the world have sought Albert's 'amateur' observational data obtained by his homemade telescope and his greatest legacy is over half a million highly accurate observations of stars' variance in brightness. It's a milestone that nobody else has reached before; in one year Jones made 13,000 published observations. His visual brightness estimates are exceptionally precise, and his unrivalled accuracy is trusted by professional astronomers and institutions worldwide.

He was awarded an Officer of the Order of the British Empire (OBE; understatedly reported in the New Zealand newspapers as being 'for services to astronomy') in 1987 and received an honorary doctorate of science (from Victoria University, Wellington) in recognition of his contribution to astronomical programmes. His work has also been honoured and acknowledged by the Smithsonian Astronomical Observatory and the British Astronomical Association.

In 1988 the minor planet 3152 was named after Albert Jones by its discoverers, and when asked if another planet could be named after him, Albert gallantly suggested it be named after his wife; minor planet 9171 is thus now named Carlyndiane.

In an interview, Jones urged all those interested in the night skies to take up variance observation:

If one has access to a modern telescope with all the bells and whistles, please have a go at variable star observing. But do not despair if you do not have such equipment, as so much needs to be done and can be accomplished with very modest gear. I know—been there, done that. The main thing is to have fun.

## BEATRICE MURIEL HILL TINSLEY 1941-81

*First to provide data and arguments that suggest*
*an expanding universe*

She has been called the most outstanding female scientist of the twentieth century and her work is acknowledged and commemorated in the United States, yet few New Zealanders have heard of Beatrice Tinsley, the pioneering cosmologist who helped change the way we think about the universe.

Best known for her work on galaxy evolution, Beatrice's short life was an ongoing determined struggle to be recognised as a scientist and astronomical theorist.

Beatrice Hill was born in Chester, England, in 1941. Her mother was a writer and her father was an Anglican preacher. When Beatrice was five she moved with her family to New Zealand and eventually settled in New Plymouth, where Beatrice's father was mayor for three years.

Ten-year-old Beatrice's bedroom walls were covered in charts for ballet, music, and diagrams of geometric shapes. At school she excelled at mathematics, languages, music and writing. Her extracurricular life was also full with ballet, pony club and piano practice; Beatrice even played violin for the National Youth Orchestra for two years. (This required a lot of practice, which Beatrice would diligently attend to, one summer even taking the violin on a family holiday to Lake Taupo, and practising her music by heading into the bush with her violin and two pegs—in order to hang her music from a branch.)

Knuckling down to whatever job was at hand, the dark-haired Beatrice was given the nickname Beetle, a name which stuck. By the age of fourteen, Beatrice had decided that she wanted to be an astrophysicist—a decision going against the norms of what a young woman should aim for in the 1950s and one that also reveals her passion, optimism, determination and intellect. In the fifth form, Beatrice asked to borrow seventh-form physics books from her teacher, who later said, 'Very occasionally you realise that you are dealing with a great mind that is infinitely superior to your own. Beatrice came into that category.'

The headmistress encouraged Beatrice to follow in her older sister's footsteps towards getting a BA—but urged Beatrice to focus on English rather than science or mathematics. Beatrice disagreed and was determined to delve more into maths, a subject that no other student at

New Plymouth Girls' High School had gone further in than the fifth form. The headmistress demurred and arranged for Beatrice to attend the boys' high school for maths and science. Beatrice would hand in a science paper about one quarter the length of the others, yet it would be concisely accurate and detailed. Beatrice gained her Junior Scholarship and, in 1957, she graduated as dux of her high school and headed to the University of Canterbury where she was one of few women at that time to study mathematics, physics and chemistry.

In her first year at Canterbury she wrote in a letter home: 'I realise that all advances in science have been made by people who have thought along totally unconventional lines and haven't been misled by the authority of that Great Name having said it was true'. When maths lectures would cover ground that she already knew, Beatrice decided:

> to sit back on lectures and work on stuff that's going to get me somewhere, namely learning new maths. Also instead of just sticking to the syllabus work in Chem and Physics I'm reading and learning as much as I can about everything.

Beatrice completed her BSc, and in 1962 achieved an MSc with first-class honours in physics, and also married a fellow research student, Brian Tinsley, who completed a PhD in atmospheric science.

Brian was offered a post at a lab for earth and planetary sciences in Dallas, Texas, and Beatrice hoped to work with a Dallas group who were investigating theoretical general relativity (Einstein's theory of gravitation, applicable to cosmology).

But macho Dallas was blind to Beatrice's potential and she struggled to find work there, ending up taking a job at the University of Texas at Austin, 320 kilometres away. There she enrolled in a PhD—being the first woman to study in the astronomy department—and finished her thesis, described as 'extraordinary and profound', in record time with the highest marks ever in the department. Her self-esteem had taken a battering and she wasn't terribly confident that her thesis would be passed; she needn't have worried, receiving marks of 99 per cent and 100 per cent.

Not one to shirk away from a challenge, Beatrice typed her own thesis. Having just adopted a child, she reasoned that it was quicker and cheaper than dressing the baby, visiting a typist and explaining the things she needed written up or changed in the thesis. She also regularly commuted between Austin and Dallas for the family to be together.

Her work overturned the previously accepted method of determining distances between galaxies, and she thus changed the accepted thought of the size, age and rate of expansion of the universe.

In the early 1900s, the scope of the known universe extended to not far beyond the edge of the Milky Way. In 1948, when Beatrice was seven, it was believed that the universe existed in a steady state of no growth. In the mid-1960s, the generally accepted Big Bang theory blew steady-state theory out of the cosmos, but it was still thought that every galaxy was exactly the same age and never increased in size—that dying stars were replaced by new material at exactly the same rate.

In her thesis, Beatrice divided the continuous life of a galaxy into ten to twenty generations, then divided each generation into twelve classes of stars. Stars with approximately the same mass will have similar lifetimes, brightnesses, and temperatures (apparent as colours). By comparing the generational gap and class differences between the groups, Beatrice theorised the time-history of a model galaxy by taking into account its luminosity, colour, chemical composition, and residual gas mass.

Although she was a tutor, Beatrice had to study with the graduate students in a tiny office, and even though she eventually received recognition from some circles, she struggled to get it. Recognition for Beatrice's work didn't come until later, when it was acknowledged by most of the astronomical community as a major advance. In showing that galaxies differed from each other and differed by varying amounts, she proved that galaxies evolve in calculable ways and that this is important.

Now with two youngsters, Beatrice put science aside for a few years to tend to the children. But without a strong support network, like many mums trying to get back to work, Beatrice struggled to get the recognition or even a foot in the door that she deserved, and her academic career was effectively shut down at this point.

In 1974, she was awarded the Annie J Canon Prize from the American Astronomical Society for her contributions to astronomy (Annie Canon was an American astronomer who had made the first serious attempt to organise and classify stars based on their temperatures). She was pleased that she was 'now an accepted member of the community of cosmologists and astrophysicists—gratifying long dreams! The work is a pleasure to me!'

Despite the fact that she had produced some of the most influential astronomical research of the times, in 1974, the University of Dallas still ignored her applications to work for them, and did not even respond to Beatrice's letter of application to be considered for the head of its astronomy department. The irony was that for the previous few years, Beatrice had worked on a part-time unpaid basis to build up the university's astronomy department.

She tried to think around this rejection, but still found it '[h]ard to explain! I am a good scientist, and among my peers treated like a full and respectable person and feel of worth. UTD has kept me at the nearest possible level to nothing and there is no one who knows enough about astronomy to care in the least for my work.'

Beatrice's hand was forced to make the decision between staying with her husband in Dallas where she had been rejected, or following her mind and her science. She chose the latter, and the heart-wrench that this caused her and the family cannot be even guessed at.

Thankfully, not all university administrations were as short-sighted as Dallas, and she became a loved and respected professor at Yale. In August 1978, Beatrice was invited to become the first female professor of astronomy at Yale, supervising and mentoring PhD students. She loved the work, found it stimulating and was also able to fit in her own research around the role.

That same year, she discovered a lump on her leg which was diagnosed as a malignant melanoma. Beatrice underwent extensive radiation and chemotherapy to try to resist the skin cancer. Although she lost the ability to write with her right hand through treatment of cancerous lymph nodes, Beatrice retrained herself to use her left, and continued her research and publishing scientific papers until her death at age 40 in 1981.

Five years after her death, the American Astronomical Society established the Beatrice M. Tinsley Prize for outstanding creative contributions to astronomy or astrophysics. Eight years later, the University of Texas at Austin established from endowment the Beatrice M. Tinsley Centennial Visiting Professorship.

Back in New Zealand, Wellington's Circa Theatre produced a play in 2005 called Bright Star, about the life of Beatrice, and in 2009 the Physics and Astronomy Department of the University of Canterbury established the Beatrice Tinsley Institute, which encompasses programmes for astronomy and astrophysics research. In 2010 the New Zealand Geographic Board officially graced a mountain in Fiordland's Kepler Mountains (named for the 17th-century German astronomer Johannes Kepler) with Beatrice's name, it is now known as Mt Tinsley (see also Mount Pickering, page 24).

Beatrice Tinsley's courage and determination in such a male-dominated world is worthwhile noting, and her importance in setting up the model for galactic evolution, which has become a cornerstone of modern cosmology, should not be undervalued or overlooked. Men such as Ernest Rutherford have long been in our history books and it's time women got a bit more of a look in.

In 2006, Christine Cole Catley (see page 90) wrote a much acclaimed official biography of Beatrice. The history of this bright star of New Zealand scientific thought is definitely worth further and deeper reading.

# MAURICE HUGH FREDERICK WILKINS 1916–2004

*First to fathom deoxyribonucleic acid*

Maurice Wilkins, born in Pongaroa in the Tararua district, was one-quarter of the team who first unravelled the mystery and double helix structure of DNA.

At the age of six, Maurice Wilkins emigrated with his family to England. He earned his PhD from the University of Birmingham in 1940 and started his career in nuclear physics. After the Second World War, he regretted his involvement in the development and the subsequent use of the atomic bomb so he turned his scientific mind to solving biological problems.

The importance of DNA as a carrier of life's genetic code was as yet unrealised until one day, peering into his microscope, Maurice Wilkins noticed a thin fibre of drawn out DNA while he was touching a gel preparation with a glass stirring rod. The implication of this was that DNA molecules were arranged in a regular fashion.

Wilkins along with Rosalind Franklin, a gifted chemist, developed X-ray diffraction photographs of DNA. (Rosalind died in 1958 at the age of 37 almost certainly due to overexposure to X-ray radiation.) From the photos, Wilkins was able to determine the distance across the double helix and the length of one turn of this helix.

Wilkins and the more famous Francis Crick and James Watson were awarded the Nobel Prize for Physiology or Medicine in 1962 'for their discoveries concerning the molecular structure of nucleic acids and its significance for information transfer in living material'.

Wilkins' other research contributed to the scientific understanding of phosphorescence, isotope separation, optical microscopy and X-ray diffraction, and to the development of radar. He died at the age of 87, but not before publishing his autobiography, *The Third Man of the Double Helix*, in 2003, where he stated:

> In the time of my parents, before World War One, most people who came to New Zealand from Europe were the more enterprising people; the people who were stronger mentally. It takes a certain amount of imagination to make a life on the other side of the world, the same imagination it takes to climb the tallest mountain.

A monument in honour of Wilkins, featuring the double helix, sits proudly on the main street of Pongaroa.

# 3

# GROUNDBREAKING NEED FOR SPEED

## MOTORING TRAILBLAZER 1874–1965

Cecil Walkden Wood was born in 1874 in Timaru. His interest in engineering was sparked from seeing one of the first steam trains in Canterbury when he was five (see page 54)—and he became enraptured by steam, grease and moving parts. By the age of sixteen he had designed and built rudimentary steam engines.

Like Henry Ford, who built his first car (the quadricycle) in 1896, Cecil started his career working in bicycles. He was an apprentice at the Tourist Cycle Works in Christchurch, and then started his own cycle business in Timaru when he was 21. Bicycles were all the rage while Cecil was in his teens. In a radio interview in the 1960s, Cecil said:

Cecil Walkden Wood in his third home-built car. The passenger is Cecil's son, Cecil Walkden Wood Junior (1902-91)

You wouldn't think that there was a fashion in bicycles, but there was, there was a fashion, and people used to discuss their bicycles heaps. They'd be in clumps, discussing what this was and that was. They knew nothing about it, but even so everyone had his own idea . . .

It's probably a good thing that Cecil isn't around in this day when men and women gather together and have the same conversations—but are now sheathed in Lycra.

Cecil learnt to temper steel in order to keep it from twisting under pressure. He bought a drill and rented a lathe, and after reading up about case hardening (baking carbon into the steel) from English magazines, built a furnace and started working on attaching engines to bicycles. At a time when mechanical parts weren't standardised, and Cecil had no instructions on how to construct the gears or work out the proportions, he built New Zealand's first motorcycle in 1895 after 'much difficulty, much trial, and much waste of good time'.

Then bicycle tubes changed in standard size, so Cecil was left with extra parts and decided to make a three-wheel belt-driven motorised vehicle in 1897. He built the chassis and a 2-horsepower engine, struggled with a carburettor (he should have got in touch with Ernest Godward— see page 56), and even investigated using a gunpowder mixture instead of petrol to fuel his contraption. Cecil's three-wheeled vehicle, however, had a tendency to veer to the left and he could only turn to the right if he let the rear wheel skid.

The first days of motoring were a dangerous time for this new pursuit, and, while New Zealand was under British law, regulations such as a speed limit of 4 miles per hour (6.5 kilometres per hour) with someone running (or riding a horse) in front of a vehicle waving a red flag were not strictly imposed. They were, however, taken as a guide, and Cecil Wood was often stopped by police for breaking the speed limit. Cecil's encounters with the local constabulary meant that he was forced off the public roads, but he was allowed to use a railway road and he tried out his vehicles there.

On 19 February 1898 two Benz cars arrived into Wellington aboard the SS *Rotomahana*, which had been imported from Paris by Liberal Party MP William McLean. The next four-wheeled imported vehicle arrived nearly two years later, and in 1903, 153 cars and motorbikes were imported.

Cecil Wood went on to produce in 1903 a four-wheel, two-seater car with a rear mounted motor and a half speed gear for hill climbing. He made a few other models after this. His claim to being the first person to locally build a car is disputed by those who believe that Frederick Dennison, an Oamaru mechanical engineer, designed and built New Zealand's first indigenous motor car in 1900. Dennison reportedly drove the vehicle from Christchurch to Oamaru in July 1900. It was an arduous journey, taking five days to ford rivers and counter numerous mechanical failures, not to mention very poor roads. For a modern car, this distance would take around three and a half hours. The return journey was too much for Dennison's car and it exploded and was destroyed by the ensuing fire. Dennison was unharmed and it is unrecorded if he built any more cars.

Cecil, Frederick and other petrolheads of the time had to contend with policemen who were always 'troubling' them about the noise, as well as dogs trying to bite the wheels and horses shying away from their cars' commotion. In 1900, the *Timaru Herald* reported the first motor car, owned by a Mr Nicholas Oates, in the South Island:

> Mr Oates' motor car was run about the streets for some time yesterday, and attracted a great deal of attention from people going about, and shopkeepers left their counters to have a look at the novelty, and the remarks made about it were mostly of a favourable character, though naturally there were those who were prepared to criticise its construction, its appearance as odd, its progression as noisy. It did not strike us as very noisy, and certainly not as odd. If one saw a man on a modern bicycle now for the first time, that would indeed be an odd sight, but a buggy without a horse is only in part a novelty . . . What did strike us about it, was the immense improvement that would be made in the cleanliness of the town if all vehicles were horseless. It is driven by a tiny gas engine, the gas being a light oil called petroline, vaporised by the heat from the engine exhaust, and ignited by electric sparks supplied by a small storage battery . . . The wheels have solid rubber tyres two inches wide; pneumatic tyres are often used, but Mr Oates doubts their safety. The wheels are of small diameter, and this brings out prominently the unevenness of the streets. Probably the regular user of the motor car becomes accustomed to the vibration, but the running over uneven roads must be hard on the vehicle.
>
> —*Timaru Herald*, 30 November 1900

Having a flash car led to another Kiwi first for Mr Oates; he was the first person convicted for speeding in a motor vehicle, and was brought before the Christchurch Magistrates Court on 15 May 1901. Oates was accused of driving down Lincoln Road 'at a speed greater than four miles an hour' and this 'excessive speed frightened the horses of Mr George Gould whose carriage was near the hospital'.

Witnesses stated that the car was driven past 'at a speed of at least ten miles per hour'. Oates, along with his business partner Alexander Lowry, owned the largest bicycle factory in the South Pacific in the late 1890s and obviously knew a thing or two about gears. He argued that the maximum speed of his two-gear vehicle was 14 miles an hour, but he claimed that he'd only been in first gear, which could only attain half that speed. It was reported in *The Star*, 15 May 1901:

> He was positive that the maximum-speed he had attained between the corner of Tuam Street and Lincoln Road and Antigua Street was not more than seven miles an hour. He admitted travelling about thirteen miles an hour along the Lincoln End itself.

The horse groom stated that 'the car passed so quickly that he could not see how many persons were therein'. (For those who aren't used to imperial measures, it's probably worth noting here that ten miles an hour equates to 16 kilometres per hour.)

Nicholas Oates was fined 20 shillings and costs. If you visit the southern hemisphere's largest private car museum—the Southward Car Museum in Paraparaumu—you will see Nicholas Oates' Benz 'velo comfortable' on display.

The first known fatal crash in New Zealand was on 12 September 1906 when Mrs Janet Meikle—described in the papers as 'an expert driver'—lost control of her vehicle on a steep and narrow gravel road to her property in a Timaru gully. The car overturned and trapped Mrs Meikle underneath, and she died. Her husband was also in the car, but survived with a broken hip.

The first New Zealand driver's licence was issued in Wellington in 1912, but licences weren't compulsory until 1925. The Motor Vehicle Act was passed in 1905 and required owners to register and licence their vehicles. The first penalties for dangerous driving came into effect in 1924. New Zealand achieved a Commonwealth first when in 1928 third-party insurance was introduced.

Drunk driving existed long before the first cars came to New Zealand. One of the first recorded instances went before the Supreme Court on 16 November 1863. Mr W Watts, a licensed hackney carriage driver—the nineteenth century equivalent to a taxi driver—from Nelson was charged with being drunk while 'driving in his machine, and also with cruelty to his horse, which it was alleged was severely abused and overdriven, and at the same time improperly fed'. Mr Watts was fined £1 for being drunk while in charge of his horse and vehicle, and for mistreating his horse his practising licence was taken from him.

On 13 March 1905, the *Press* recorded that a party of Auckland motorists had just completed a trip from Greymouth, via the Otira Gorge, 'a route not previously gone over by motor-car, and a tour considered by many motorists an impossible one to successfully accomplish'. The 15-horsepower Darracq's passengers were Mr and Mrs WB Leyland, and Mr and Mrs JA Moody.

> The party motored from Auckland to Wellington, via Rotorua, Napier, and the Rimutakas, and then crossed to Nelson where their tour of the South Island commenced. Between Nelson and Greymouth the journey occupied two days, and they found the roads fairly good, but in a chronic state of repair . . . Some difficulties were experienced in crossing the unbridged rivers, but with the aid of a wire rope and block and tackle, which they carried with them, they were able to haul the car through with the ladies in it. The appearance of the car created quite a sensation, being the first seen by many in the districts through which they passed. Just before reaching Reefton they saw a cyclist on ahead, and tootled their alarm. The unusual noise caused the cyclist to turn round, and either the strange vehicle that met his view or having turned too sharply caused him to fall off.

A few years later, in January 1907, WB Leyland set out from Wellington on the first round-trip of the North Island by car. To cater to this new craze, which was soon to become a way of life, petrol (then called benzene) was sold in 4-gallon (18-litre) tins by blacksmiths and grocers. The first petrol stations were installed in 1926, while the first traffic lights came into operation on 1 June 1947 in Auckland.

The first oil field to be discovered in New Zealand was at the Motouoa field in New Plymouth port area in 1866—it produced around 50 gallons of oil a week.

Fifty years before the 'girls can do anything' catchphrase, Sybil Audrey Marie Lupp (1916–1994) was New Zealand's first female mechanic, working on top-of-the-line Jaguars and making them purr. She was also a keen motor-racing driver, garage proprietor and motor vehicle dealer. As a member of the Association of New Zealand Car Clubs, Sybil set a New Zealand record for 1100–1500cc cars in the flying kilometre from 75 to 100.52 mph in 1951; the record stood until 1957.

## FIRST VEHICLE TO THE SOUTH POLE

Sir Ed Hillary is part of our national psyche; the beekeeper who—along with Sherpa Tenzing Norgay—was the first in the world to reach the summit of the 8847-metre (29,028 foot) Mount Everest in 1953. However, not that many people know that he was also the first to drive a motor vehicle to the South Pole. Not only that—but the vehicle of choice for the Trans-Antarctic Expedition was a modified Massey Ferguson tractor—how Kiwi can you get?

The party of five arrived at the pole on 4 January 1958; it had taken the three tractors, caboose and two sledges more than 80 days to complete the 1930-kilometre journey. Sir Ed's Antarctic party was also the first to have reached the pole since Captain Robert F Scott's expedition in 1912.

During the gruelling expedition they encountered white-out conditions and soft snow the consistency of sugar—which made progress difficult and burned more fuel. Sir Ed was in radio contact with Scott Base and, prior to spotting the black blob of the South Pole tower, he reported, 'We are heading hellbent for the Pole. God willing and crevasses permitting . . . It is tough, but not too tough'. At times, members of the New Zealand team had to resort to using shovels to clear a path for the tractors, and by the time they arrived at the Pole they only had one drum of petrol left—32 kilometres' worth of fuel. After making their tractor pilgrimage to the Pole, the expedition members slept for 16 hours and were sent a congratulatory message by Prime Minister Walter Nash.

For his adventures and his humanitarian efforts, Sir Ed is perhaps the best known New Zealander to have ever lived. Hillary also took a jetboat journey up the Ganges River in 1977 (see the Hamilton jetboat on page 192). Sir Edmund Hillary died in Auckland on 11 January 2008, aged 88. He was farewelled at a state funeral—an unprecedented honour for a private citizen.

At the alpine centre on New Zealand's highest mountain, Aoraki/ Mount Cook, there is a statue of Sir Ed on the Hillary Deck looking out to the 3754-metre mountain. Ascending the mountain's notoriously difficult south face was Edmund Hillary's first great mountaineering achievement, and the Southern Alps were the training ground for his Everest and Antarctic expeditions.

## FIRST TRACTORS

The first tractors to work New Zealand farms were imported in 1904. However, the machines—an Ivel and a Kinnard-Haines—were so large and heavy that their ability to adequately perform the tasks they were needed for was negligible. There were only 136 tractors in the whole country in 1919, the Ferguson system—which allowed other farm tools to be attached to tractors by means of a hydraulic connection—revolutionised farm work from the late 1940s. Tractors reached their peak of pastoral popularity in 1971 when more than 96,500 tractors were hard at work on the nation's farms.

## FIRST TRAINS

New Zealand's first public steam-powered railway was opened in 1863 at Ferrymead with the line servicing ships and running to Christchurch. These were the days when a first was celebrated before the fact; when the first sod was turned on the Temuka to Timaru section of the main trunkline in 1871, hundreds of people gathered and the day had an air of a public holiday.

The establishment of a nationwide rail system linking all the main centres together was a priority of Julius Vogel—eighth premier of New Zealand and sci-fi writer (see *Anno Domini*, page 232).

The first train to travel the length of the North Island main trunkline, the 'Parliament Special' left Wellington on 7 August 1908 and arrived in Auckland twenty and a half hours later. The train of twelve carriages was carrying almost all of the nation's MPs as well as Prime Minister Joseph Ward who were on their way to greet an American navy contingent. There were no sleeping berths and some of the MPs slept in chairs (like a few do in Parliament these days), others made up beds on the floor. It was not a smooth ride, with some delays put down to pumice dust getting into the axles. In February 1909 an 'express' service was introduced, which made the trip in eighteen hours.

## FIRST LAND-SPEED RECORD FOR A 68-YEAR-OLD BIKIE

On 26 August 1967 an Invercargill chap by the name of Burt Munro claimed the world land-speed record class under 1000cc at Speed Week on the Bonneville Salt Flats in Utah. His average speed that day was 183.586 miles per hour (one way 190.07 miles per hour). This record still stands to this very day. He was the first 68-year-old to achieve any such speed record, and the first to do so on a bike he had tinkered with for twenty-odd years. Burt's motto was, 'I'll never give up until I've had a good run.'

# ERNEST R GODWARD 1869–1936

*First New Zealander to make his fortune from the head of a pin
and bring the Kiwi entrepreneurial spirit to the world*

*First to make refined energy go further*

Sometimes the smallest things can make you wealthy. Ernest Godward's wealth came about because of hairpins. He noticed that the pins used by women in the late nineteenth century weren't very good at doing their job—keeping hair in place. To rectify this, Godward designed 'an ingenious little contrivance', a spiral hairpin that could be put in the hair but would not work itself backwards and was unlikely to slip without being deliberately taken out.

This tiny patented invention (the rights of which were sold for the impressive sum of £20,000 in 1901) was taken up worldwide, lining Godward's pockets and paving the way for further inventions including improvements to post-hole borers and inkwells, burglar-proof windows, a better egg-beater and an efficient carburettor that revolutionised the internal combustion engine.

Life didn't start out terribly well for London-born Ernest. He was a sickly child and unable to start school until he was nine years old. He didn't last long there and ran away to sea when he was twelve, working on a vessel that took him to Japan. The British Consul sent him back to London and he trained as a mechanic for a fire-engine manufacturer

Dragon float at the Invercargill Cycling Club Carnival (c. 1910)
with the irrepressible E R Godward in the mouth of the dragon

in London. The travel bug hit Godward again, and when he was fifteen he took on odd tasks on board a P&O passenger ship—becoming the vessel's 'napkin folding champion'—which led to further sea voyages, eventually washing up at Port Chalmers, Dunedin, in 1886.

The years at sea seemed to have strengthened Ernest's constitution, and in Dunedin he started accruing sporting achievements, becoming a champion swimmer, runner, rower and cyclist. Cycles were new to the country, and Godward's mechanical training helped establish him as a partner at the Southland Cycle Works when he moved to Invercargill.

He married, and started creating a family of ten children with his wife. Requiring money to support this growing family and not getting enough financial nor intellectual stimulation from his day job, Ernest started inventing—the non-slip hairpin, the non-slip egg-beater that could prepare eggs for a sponge cake in under three and a half minutes, when other beaters did it in fifteen, a new type of hair curler, a hedge-trimmer made from bicycle parts and many other useful implements. A bit of a Renaissance man, Ernest, whose landscapes were sought after, enjoyed painting, played the banjo and the ocarina, and was an avid collector of books, and a great public speaker who performed with a whimsical Invercargill club of people who were 'not disposed to hide their light under a bushel'. He was elected as an Invercargill councillor, continued his sporting participation, and had a sixteen-bedroom house built for his large family. Possibly because of having so many doors in his house, Godward also invented the padded draught protector—still seen in many an old house nationwide.

Godward expanded his talents to customising motorbikes, adding his own fuel economiser. Finding that the economiser also worked in cars, he started importing automobiles and fitting his new invention to them—which made a motor engine more powerful because the explosion of fuel was bigger thus minimising the waste of fuel. He also won the Invercargill to Dunedin motor race in a car fitted with his economiser.

The innovative device was a curved chamber that caught drops of liquid fuel and turned them into vapour before they reached the cylinders.

He tried to sell this invention to engineers in the British motor-car industry and they were interested in fitting Godward's invention to London buses, but a contract fell through. It is difficult to not surmise that this lack of support was because the British were wary of an upstart from the colonies who had no formal engineering training. Not to be put off, Ernest returned to New Zealand and took up engineering study, also developing his economiser into 72 models.

He moved to New York and managed to sell his 'Godward Vaporiser' invention to the US Army. There, bootleg whisky, gin, brandy and rum were used in testing the fuel economy of Godward's vaporiser, and it was found that it greatly increased the power—by up to 15 per cent—of all army trucks. It was urged that the device should be installed in all army vehicles 'in view of war-time eventualities'.

The city of Philadelphia had it fitted in 580 buses and 3000 taxis in 1929, the financial benefit of which helped Godward survive the stockmarket crash. By the 1930s, Godward was recognised as a world authority on the internal-combustion engine, and his advice and business sense were well respected. He set up a manufacturing business in New York which he advertised as being in the business of 'Power, Efficiency, Economy'.

Off the coast of Gibraltar, on a boat headed back to Invercargill, 69-year-old Godward participated in and won an on board skipping competition, but collapsed and died immediately after. He over-achieved to the last.

Many people credit him with the invention of the familiar egg-beater seen in many Kiwi kitchens, however, this is a misstatement of the truth. Ernest didn't invent the egg-beater that we envisage, but a different egg-beater, which was to aid in the development of later models. His super-fast egg-beater had a suction pad at the bottom of the blade shaft so it would stick to the bowl. Ernest certainly developed a better egg-beater, but his real legacy was that of a self-made man bringing the Kiwi entrepreneurial spirit to the world; his fuel economiser is the basis for the modern-day carburettor, and his solving a simple problem of hairdressing helped him do that.

## MOUNTAIN BUGGY—A KIWI INVENTION, COMBINING BABY CARE AND EXERCISE

Allan Croad was a New Zealand dad who wanted to go jogging (see Arthur Lydiard, page 105) while looking after his young son. Pushing the conventional heavy and not very agile pushchair while on the run was too cumbersome and not an option. Croad wanted a buggy, not a stroller, so being a resourceful bloke, he combined a child's car seat with a golf trundler to create the 'buggy'. This mock-up was more than adequate for the job, and Croad realised that he had a buggy that would cater to New Zealand's outdoors lifestyle. The larger tyres enabled access to off-road terrain and the lightweight aluminium frame meant it was easy to push without exerting too much extra effort. Croad pitched it to a manufacturing company, and in 1992 the Mountain Buggy was launched. Being lighter, stronger and easier to steer and fold than traditional prams, it was a top seller in New Zealand and soon conquered the world. The buggy was honoured on a New Zealand Post Clever Kiwis stamp in 2007. The original prototype of the buggy is on exhibit at MOTAT, and you can see new generations of the Mountain Buggy at nearly every café and wheeling the pavements of the western world.

# BUNGY JUMPING

Bungy jumping is more about not breaking ground, but its development as a tourist attraction is a groundbreaking achievement. Mention the word bungy, and many international visitors will immediately associate the word with New Zealand.

Legend has it that a woman on Vanuatu's Pentecost Island was the first land-diver/bungy jumper. Climbing up a banyan tree in order to escape her cruel husband, she leapt from the tree to evade him after he followed her up. She landed on the ground below unscathed. Not wanting to be outdone by his wife, he also leapt, but had failed to notice that she had tied a vine to her ankles, thus preventing the calamity that befell him.

This Vanuatu legend is commemorated annually during the yam festival season on Pentecost Island, and sees local men and boys as young

First leaps of faith: a woman doing a
A J Hackett bungy jump at Skippers
Canyon, Otago, 3 August 1992

as seven jump from a 20–30-metre high man-made tower with only a vine attached to their legs. The practice, filmed by David Attenborough in the 1950s, is called *nagol*, or 'land-diving', and it inspired members of the Oxford University Dangerous Sports Club in the 1970s to tie a rope to their ankles and fling themselves from heights, filming their experimental jumps.

In the 1980s, Kiwi AJ Hackett saw these films, and decided that it wasn't beyond the realm of possibility to develop this adventurous activity and encourage people to pay money to partake in such madness. Along with his friend and fellow Kiwi adrenaline junkie Henry van Asch, and with the help of Auckland University scientists, Hackett experimented with latex rubber cords, making the first jump from Auckland's Greenhithe bridge in 1986. AJ and friends then made a series of experimental extreme jumps from a ski area gondola, 91 metres above the snow in Tignes, France, in 1987.

Naming the activity after the stretchy cords that secured their surfboards to the tops of their cars, AJ, Henry and their mates did extensive testing on the cords and decided that they needed to confirm their absolute faith (and some would say, insanity) in the safety and predictability of their bungy system in a very public manner.

In June 1987, AJ went up the Eiffel Tower, managing to evade security overnight, and at dawn the next day performed the world's first public bungy jump. He was immediately arrested by Parisian police, but released minutes later, adding to the phenomenal PR coup that made international headlines.

Not paying much heed to the sceptics who said that bungy jumping was a fad with very little commercial viability that would never catch on, they set up the world's first commercial bungy operation at Queenstown's Kawarau Bridge in November 1988.

The first Department of Conservation (DoC) licence was granted for 30 days and that year, 28 people paid $75 each to bungy off the 43-metre high bridge. With rigorous safety standards and practice guidelines, the AJ Hackett franchise of this extreme sport has helped several million people challenge themselves by leaping from a tall structure while connected to a large elastic cord. This hair-raising Kiwi invention has helped place New Zealand on the map of adventure tourism and market the values of New Zealanders—outdoor lifestyle, quality, reliability and trust, with a dollop of craziness for good measure.

# ALEXANDER McKAY 1841–1917

*First to suggest lateral movement—groundwork*

*First to develop the telephoto lens*

Alexander McKay's austere upbringing in a Scottish farming family was good groundwork for an adult career as a nineteenth-century exploration geologist in the rugged, mountainous, bush-clad terrain of New Zealand.

The man who was to become a famous pioneering geologist sailed from Glasgow to New Zealand, arriving in Bluff in 1863 when he was 22 years old. McKay tried his hand as an agricultural worker, then as an Otago gold prospector; by 1883, McKay had established himself as a trusted field geologist within the Geological Survey, and, despite having very little schooling, had published 50 scientific papers and demonstrated a keen eye for the structure and geological history of the land.

In the 1880s the scientific community believed that the only way the Earth's faultlines moved was vertically, however, after the 1889 earthquake at Glen Wye (on the Lewis Pass Highway, near Hanmer Springs), Alexander McKay carefully measured the horizontal displacement of two fencelines and was the first to record horizontal movement during an earthquake. Mountains had been built by the uplift of land by repeated small fault movements over a long period of time. From this observation, McKay deduced that the forming of New Zealand's mountains had occurred much more recently (in the last 10 million years) than elsewhere in the documented world.

This was—excuse the pun—groundbreaking thinking and—like many new ideas—it wasn't well received by traditionally educated scientists. Sadly it wasn't until the 1930s and 1940s with aerial photography that the full significance of McKay's observations were understood.

The beauty of New Zealand's Southern Alps is a product of the sideways movement of adjacent sections of the Earth's crust along the Alpine Fault (one of the world's largest faults). Sometimes these sections can move laterally by hundreds of kilometres; in Glen Wye the fencelines had moved by 2.6 metres.

Also in the late 1880s, when he was in his forties, McKay took up the new hobby of photography. Experimenting with camera and telescope design he was interested in getting the best possible definition from his camera and even ground down bottle ends to make his own lenses.

Combining optical parts from opera glasses and a telescope, McKay discovered he could create a long-focus lens capable of capturing the detail of the gun ports and rigging lines of a Russian warship anchored in Wellington harbour, about two and a half kilometres away. Paparazzi around the globe now use this process to provide weekly updates on what celebrities are eating for lunch.

This May 1886 photograph—and evidence of the first telephoto lens—of the ship *Vjestnik*, along with others of Alexander McKay's are stored at the Alexander Turnbull Library in Wellington.

Alexander McKay, the folk hero of New Zealand geology, also wrote poetry and was said to enjoy a bit of whisky with his Scotch oats. He assembled over 100,000 fossil collections, which still stand as fine examples and form the core of the national fossil collection held at GNS Science headquarters. The self-educated explorer who rose to become government geologist was a pioneer and his work helped New Zealand to become a leader in neotectonics—the study of the motions and contortions of the Earth's crust.

## DR BILL ROBINSON 1938–2011

*To counter lateral movement, enter another Kiwi first*

Dr Bill Robinson was a physicist who worked for the Department of Scientific and Industrial Research (DSIR) and in the 1970s came up with the idea of shock absorbers for buildings. He invented and developed the base isolation technique where a structure is not built into the ground, but rests on flexible bearings known as base isolators. In the event of an earthquake, these can reduce and absorb the seismic energy transferred to the structure by up to 80 per cent, meaning that the horizontal movement of a building relative to the ground will be minimal and controlled.

The world's first building to be mounted on lead-rubber bearings was the William Clayton building on Molesworth Street in Wellington in 1982 (this innovative building also was installed with a solar water-heating system). The whole structure, including the basement, is supported on 80 lead-rubber bearings and in an earthquake the building can move up to 150 millimetres horizontally, thereby minimising potential for structural damage.

This system can also be used on bridges and other structures that are prone to experiencing the dynamic forces of nature. Many strategic or valuable buildings—such as government headquarters and Te Papa— have been built with base isolators. In this way, Dr Bill Robinson has safeguarded people and our heritage.

The effectiveness of lead-rubber bearings was demonstrated in the devastating earthquakes that occurred in Christchurch between September 2010 and June 2011; Christchurch Women's Hospital was the only building in that city that had been built with lead-rubber bearings, and it was able to continue operating without any problems.

During the severe 1994 Los Angeles earthquake, the University of Southern California Teaching Hospital, protected by lead-rubber bearings, remained operational while the ten other hospitals in the area were so badly damaged that they had to be evacuated. Base isolators are now mandatory in all new American hospitals.

Robinson's innovative work has been recognised with many honours, including the Rutherford Medal for Technology, an honorary DSc and a fellowship of the Royal Society of New Zealand. In 2007 he was appointed Companion of the Queen's Service Order (QSO) for services to engineering. He founded Robinson Seismic Ltd, which, after his death in 2011, continues to test and manufacture his devices.

## GROUNDBREAKERS

The first strike by New Zealand workers was in 1821 in the Bay of Islands. Maori timber workers downed tools because they wanted to be paid 'for their labour in money as was the case in England, or else in gunpowder'. They were probably being paid in food and accommodation.

# 4

# GAMES WE PLAY AND THINGS WE SAY

## FIRST WORLD FIRST IN SPORT

The first New Zealander ever to hold an athletic world best was John Hempton who ran 9 4/5 seconds for the 100 yards on 6 February 1892 at the New Zealand Championships in Christchurch. This world record was recognised by the International Amateur Athletics Federation (IAAF) as being compliant with their regulations. The 100-yard distance is the equivalent of around 91.5 metres.

Yvette Williams is the first and (so far) only New Zealand athlete, male or female, to hold a world record in a field event, having achieved a world record in the long jump event at an athletic meeting in Gisborne in 1954.

## FIRST FIFTEEN

You wouldn't believe it, but New Zealanders weren't the first to play rugby. Rugby was invented by William Webb Ellis, an Anglican clergyman, in 1823. When he was 17, and attending Rugby School in England, Ellis had run forward with a ball that he had caught during a game of football. The new game of rugby gradually spread to English universities and schools.

The story picks up halfway around the world and more than 40 years later, when, in 1867, the Speaker of New Zealand Parliament Sir David Monro of Nelson sent his sixteen-year-old son Charles 'Home' to 'finish' his schooling at Christ's College in Finchley, England. When Charles came back to New Zealand, he told of the oval football that he had been playing with in the 'homeland', and convinced the Nelson Football Club to ditch the round Gaelic ball they had been using for a soccer-like game. This new version of the game, introduced by Charlie, was played in teams of twenty and with a lighter oval ball. The aim was to touch the ball down, which gave the team the right to have a 'try' at goal—points were only accrued by kicking goals. The first recorded game of rugby in New Zealand was played in Nelson on Saturday 14 May 1870, between the Nelson club team and Nelson College. Onlookers would have had no idea that they were witnessing a first moment that sparked a New Zealand sporting tradition.

The match was reported in the Colonist newspaper later that day, on the same page was the report of 'A Large Cheese' (see page 157, cheese rolls):

Mr. Charles Knight, of Applby, has lately sent Home to his friends in Sussex, a cheese weighing 225lb5. It is the produce of the milk from thirty-seven cows, each of which was milked four times to produce the quantity required. It is a handsome, well-formed cheese, a credit to any dairy, and ought to be exhibited at some agricultural show in England, where most probabiy it would secure the first prize.

The match was reported in the *Colonist* newspaper later that day. The paper described the local community meeting at the Masonic Hall and the new ships in the harbour, eventually getting on to the first game of rugby recorded in New Zealand, held at the Botanics Reserve in Nelson, and played in front of a modest crowd of 200.

Football Match.—The College v. Town.—An enthusiastic football player sends us the following account of this game:—Saturday was the day appointed for the match of football between the College and the Town Club. The Collegians showed well in their sporting uniform, and looked well up to their work, and were decidedly the favourites amongst the outsiders . . .

The toss for the kick off having been won by the College . . . Almost as soon as the ball is amongst the Town players, the College have followed up, when a kick sends it over their heads again, and then it is seen first in one place, and then in another, the whole field in hot pursuit. Now some player runs with it, and a general scrimmage ensues; it is all shove, pull, rush, and roll about in a confused mass till 'down' is cried, and away the ball goes again till perchance it gets in touch or caught . . . Everyone seems now to be doing his best, and the ball is first one end then another, and the little College boys are winding in and out amongst the big players in the most remarkable way . . . Presently, with a cheer, the ball is kicked through the College goal by Clark, and so the game terminates in favour of the Town Club. The day was very favourable, being rather cloudy, and quite calm and the field was decorated with a fair sprinkling of ladies . . .

Canterbury founded the first rugby union in 1879, followed soon afterwards by Wellington, Otago and Auckland and the New Zealand Rugby Union was established in 1892. By the early 1880s, New Zealand had hosted a team from New South Wales, Australia, and toured there in return. The year 1904 saw the provinces competing for the Ranfurly Shield. In 1905 the first national team to be known as the All Blacks toured the United Kingdom, France and North America—which other books have written about.

## OUTDOOR BASKETBALL MAKES ITS DEBUT

The first game of basketball was also the first game of netball played in New Zealand and it took place in 1907 at the suggestion of the secretary of the Presbyterian Bible Class Union, Rev. JC Jamieson, after he saw the game being played in Australia. This 'outdoor basketball' game became popular and was soon played in schools throughout the country; by 1924 the New Zealand Basketball Association was formed to administer the game on a national basis, and the local team, the Silver Ferns, was established in 1938. The first world netball tournament was played in England in 1963, and the Silver Ferns played competitively, despite the fact that they had spent six weeks on a boat to get to the event. They narrowly lost to Australia and achieved second place.

## FIRST BOWLING OF A MAIDEN OVER

Cricket was apparently played here as early as 1835, when Charles Darwin made a visit to our shores.

On New Year's Day 1849, New Zealand's first recorded cricket match was officially played in Dunedin between single and married teams.

The All England Eleven was the first overseas cricket team to play in New Zealand, arriving in Christchurch on 31 January 1864. The not strictly English team included Australian cricket legend Tom Wills—who many sports trivia fanatics will know as one of those responsible for founding the Australian Rules version of rugby. The visitors played four games; the hosts drew one.

In Christchurch on 10 January 1930, a four-day match against England was the first time New Zealand's national cricket team played test cricket. England claimed victory by eight wickets.

# FIRST CHESS, MATE

The world's first recorded chess game by telegraph was started in June 1866 by Nelson and Christchurch clubs. The game took several months, and was won by the Christchurch team.

> The Christchurch players had the opening move, and the Nelson club were acting on the defensive from a strong attack but when, to all appearances, they were recovering themselves, and the balance of the game was becoming more evenly adjusted, an ill-considered move (we refer to the 19th) was made, from which they could not recover, and the game was, to all intents and purposes, lost.

> —*Colonist*, 14 September 1866

# BUGGER!

After scoring what is now called one of the greatest forward tries of all time, and helping to secure a significant win against the Springboks in a 1956 test series match, All Black Peter Jones had a radio broadcast microphone pushed in his face. Jones was asked the fall-back question resorted to by hack journalists the world over, 'How do you feel?'

'I'm absolutely buggered,' was his reply.

It was the first time that the term 'buggered' had been used in a national live-to-air broadcast. It certainly wasn't the last.

The term bugger can be used as an expression of surprise, or as a synonym for 'broken'. 'I'm buggered' can be used to indicate a state of fatigue.

What he meant to say was that he was exhausted. Jones had just played in front of a crowd of 61,240, and was not mindful that his words were being broadcast to the remaining 2.5 million inhibited polite Kiwis at home. Although frowned upon, his offside comment was mostly disregarded at the time, but it has made the history books because the victory was so celebrated.

It appears we may be an uncouth lot. Fifty years later, All Black skipper Richie McCaw reportedly said he was 'totally shagged' after playing most of the game on the field in a winning match against the Wallabies in Brisbane in 2006.

It seems to be one of Richie's choice phrases. He also mentioned that he was 'absolutely shagged' after leading the All Blacks to World Cup victory in 2011, and before having the world's most awkward three-way handshake with a prime minister.

Let's not forget Sir Edmund Hillary (see page 52), who after summiting Mount Everest, said to his lifelong friend George Lowe back at base camp: 'Well, George, we knocked the bastard off.'

In 1999, 120 complaints were received by the Broadcasting Standards Authority regarding the use of the word 'bugger' (including by a dog) in a humorous television commercial advertising vehicles suitable for farms. After examining dictionary and popular uses of the word, the Authority Board said, taking the issues of context, medium and audience into account, that the advertisement was unlikely to cause widespread offence. The complaints were not upheld.

Kiwi writer Ronald Hugh Morrieson once made the following tragically prophetic remark, 'I hope I'm not another one of these poor buggers who get discovered when they're dead.' See First Opening Lines (page 248) for why this was such a self-fulfilling prophecy.

## CYRIL BROWNLIE 1895–1954

*First to be sent off*

Cyril Brownlie was the first rugby player to be sent off the field in an international test. Welsh ref Albert Freethy accused the All Black forward of stomping on an English opponent in the eighth minute of the game. Cyril—one of three brothers who represented New Zealand on the rugby field—denied the accusations of foul play.

Among the crowd of some 60,000 spectators on this blustery January day in 1925 at Twickenham stadium were Edward, the Prince of Wales and the British Prime Minister Stanley Baldwin. At half-time the Prince of Wales (later to become King Edward VIII) tried to have Brownlie reinstated; possibly the first (and probably the last) occasion a royal family member has offered to intervene on behalf of the All Blacks.

The efforts of the prince couldn't engineer Cyril's return, but the team, who were given the nickname 'The Invincibles', despite being one man short for 70 minutes of the match, won 17–11. It was only the second time that the New Zealand and England sides had met; the previous occasion was in 1905 when the All Blacks had been easy victors by 15–0; and the all-conquering All Blacks were coming to the end of an unbeaten tour (their last defeat had been against the Springboks four years earlier).

Perhaps the subsequent controversy was because Cyril's sending off was an ignominious first, and an inglorious claim to fame that New Zealand would have preferred any other team to have. Within hours of the match, Freethy issued a statement justifying his decision, published in *The Times* of London:

Cyril Brownlie was the first to rile a ref at rugby

In some loose play the ball had been sent away and two or three England forwards were lying on the ground. C. Brownlie was a few feet away from them, and as he came back he deliberately kicked on the leg an England forward lying face downward on the ground. I had taken my eye off the ball for a moment, and therefore saw exactly what happened. Previous to this I had warned each side generally three times, and therefore I had no option but to send Brownlie off the field. I much regretted having to do this, but in the circumstances I had no alternative but to take this drastic action . . .

*The Times* proclaimed 'This was an unprecedented indignity in the match'.

On 5 January, two days after the match, an (New Zealand) *Evening Post* editorial dramatically stated that the event 'could not help the spirit of Imperialism', and quoted the All Black team manager SS Dean as saying, 'the referee made a mistake . . . It is felt that a grave injustice has been done to Brownlie and the unfortunate occurrence has cast a gloom over the whole party'.

The England back Leonard Corbett didn't catch the foul play, but some years later stated that he had never tried to 'establish the facts which caused the regrettable incident and have always studiously avoided being drawn into the numerous controversies that arose out of it'. Corbett agreed with the widely held view that 'Mr Freethy was the ablest, fairest and firmest referee' . . . and the sending off had the desired effect to 'steady the more exuberant and excitable players on both sides'.

A teacher by profession, Freethy was elected a life member of the Welsh Rugby Union.

Cyril Brownlie represented New Zealand on 31 occasions, scoring eleven tries. The whistle used for his red-carding is now housed in the New Zealand Rugby Museum and is used to start each World Cup.

## PIP GOULD 1940–

*First long-course swim record setter*

In one day a fifteen-year-old Auckland schoolgirl, Phillipa 'Pip' Gould, was the first (and so far only) New Zealander to set world records for long-course swimming. The St Cuthbert's College student broke the 220-yard and 200-metre backstroke records at the Newmarket pool in Auckland on 16 January 1957. She swam the 200 metres in a time of 2:39.9. The following year, she set two more records in the 100 metres (winning a bronze medal) and 110 yards backstroke at the Commonwealth Games in Cardiff. Pip had competed at the 1956 Melbourne Olympics, placing sixth at her heat in the 100-metre backstroke.

## REWI ALLEY, 路易·艾黎, LÙYÌ ÀILÍ 1897–1987

*First to introduce gung-ho to the lexicon of human relations*

*First Kiwi social reform revolutionary in China—bringing community organisations to China*

You'll often hear the phrase 'gung-ho!' Its meaning has changed over the years, as people worldwide have enthusiastically taken it up. It's heard in modern culture from sources as diverse as rocker Patti Smith and the Star Wars *Clone Wars* movie. But when Rewi Alley introduced gung-ho to the western idiom and consciousness, it was in its original meaning of 'work together'.

Born in Springfield in inland Canterbury and brought up in the notable Alley family, Rewi, like his siblings, was affected by the strong work ethic and attitude of his parents. His father was Frederick James Alley, a schoolmaster, and his mother Clara Maria Buckingham was involved in the temperance and women's rights movement. His brothers and sisters were to become variously an All Black (see Geoff Alley on page 258); a pioneering primary school teacher; a gifted engineer (credited with suggesting that the University of Canterbury should be moved out of central Christchurch and to Ilam); and a smart and efficient nursing administrator.

Named after Maori chief Rewi Maniapoto, famed for his resistance to the British forces during the Land Wars of the 1860s, Rewi was an avid reader, delighting in *Boys' Own* and classic adventure tales.

Not a stranger to the strap for various schoolboy misdeeds, Rewi was inspired by adventure and thoughts of rebellion, and so falsified his age and enlisted in the army in 1916. He served in France, was wounded twice on the battlefield and sent home with a Military Medal for Bravery.

Back home, for six years he struggled to make a living on a scrubby hilly bit of Taranaki farmland he co-owned with an old schoolmate, and the Depression years hit tough with wool prices at a low. Rewi's heart wasn't in it.

His sense of adventure was piqued by *Auckland Weekly News* reports on the 'red peril' in China. Tensions were rising between two anti-imperial factions: the communists (reds) and the *guomintang* (blues); both were fighting internationally funded suppressions to their people's uprising. Alley thought he would go and 'take a look at their revolution'. Getting work as a radio operator on a boat headed to China, he set sail for Shanghai, arriving there in early 1927.

Rewi Alley started his Chinese working career as a fireman (later fire chief inspector) in Shanghai and began to study the language. Taking day trips around Shanghai, Rewi observed the chaotic city: an affluent international metropolis still basking in the last sunset rays of British imperialism and colonialism in contrast, yet cheek to cheek, with extreme poverty with regular instances of corruption, child labour, oppression and cruelty to workers. In Shanghai he met Joseph Bailie, whose ideas about the need for schooling and other training in the villages of rural China heavily influenced Alley.

On a visit to a village to admire the springtime blossoms, Rewi saw silk workers accused of being communists and then executed in the street. He was appalled and struggled to understand the horrific events that were happening around him.

Although it went unreported by the world media at the time, widespread and catastrophic famine ravaged much of China in 1929, leaving over three million people dead. This devastation perturbed Rewi Alley and he started thinking about ways to help the Chinese people.

Rewi was appointed by the League of Nations to oversee dyke repair at Wuhan, Hubei Province, where a local governor threatened to turn machine guns on thousands of refugees fleeing the floods, simply because he viewed them as communists. Understanding that these weren't just idle threats, Rewi arranged for the refugees to be relocated to distant parts of the dyke—breaking up the large group of displaced people into smaller, manageable camps to which he arranged supplies of food and the logistics of transportation. In doing so he effectively saved the lives of hundreds of thousands of people.

Rebellion against the oppressive forces seemed to be the answer and the New Zealander, brought up in a land of democracy, started working as an underground member of the Communist Party; at one stage he was given the job of washing the blood off criminals' money confiscated by the Red Army in raids.

Rewi adopted two Chinese sons, and with the belief that education was a key to instigating social reform, he started up technical training schools.

The Japanese invaded China in force in 1937—taking advantage of the fact that most of China's industry was focused at the ports. Seeing this weakness wreak havoc on the Chinese people's ability to resist the invasion, Rewi Alley came up with a plan to bring production to the inland areas, which would also provide jobs for fleeing refugees. This revolutionary idea would be achieved through a series of Chinese Industrial Cooperatives (INDUSCO), and would be promoted with the Chinese phrase 'gung-ho', or 'work together'.

Travelling the interior of China by bike, foot, hitching lifts on the back of trucks, stowing away on trains, buses and cars, Rewi managed to set up centres for these small-scale self-supporting cooperatives.

A *Time* magazine article from April 1940 describes the many advantages of the cooperatives:

> The units were mobile, easily disguised, easily housed, and were not, like big factories, obvious targets for Japanese bombers. They supplied military needs which no other source in China could produce so efficiently … Above all they provided millions of refugees who trekked west on the heels of freedom with the hope of lasting relief in the form of jobs … Cooperatives entirely revitalized whole towns.

Importing and employing the Kiwi number-eight-wire ethos, Rewi succeeded in turning under-resourced townships and barely functioning machines into successful cooperative factories that started producing not just military munitions, trucks, irrigation equipment, boilers, cotton, cloth and blankets, but provided employment, leadership and a means of survival for all the workers.

Rewi continued to build technical training schools to prepare young people in the trades needed for the cooperatives. His main effort was in the remote Gobi desert, where he established a school but then—with the Japanese army encroaching—moved it, trekking the dismantled school and machinery 1000 kilometres inland to Shandan on the Old Silk Road in northwest Gansu province. The school's motto was 'Create and Analyse' and it encouraged cooperative effort on the shoulders of self-reliance and the development of self. Political talk was out of the question, but practical skills and teaching by doing was Rewi's gung-ho solution to arm the people with productive autonomy. He was asked to start up cooperatives in India in 1952, but declined the invite, preferring to focus on his work in China.

The importance of this grassroots democratic revolution can't be underestimated. The Four-Square or dairy co-ops may be the collectives we mostly think of in New Zealand, but this social reform and spark towards group consciousness by a Kiwi really made a vast difference to the nation that holds one fifth of the world's population.

Much of New Zealand was conservative and still uncertain over how to feel about Rewi's involvement with the communists, which led to many rubbishing him when he spoke out against American actions during the Korean War. But Rewi continued in his pragmatic pacifism and from 1953 onwards spoke on behalf of international peace agencies in China and internationally, lecturing on the need for nuclear disarmament.

He was a founder and the inspiration behind the New Zealand China Friendship Society which was established in 1958. With this diplomatic institution and the times changing with New Zealand recognising the People's Republic of China in 1972, Rewi Alley gained acceptance and received honourable recognition in his homeland, including the QSO—having earlier refused a knighthood.

In the sixties he suggested that Kiwis needed a bit of gung-ho: 'New Zealand is asleep . . . basically good, the youth of New Zealand needs challenge, a realisable object, the way to work together.'

He'd associated with Chairman Mao, and with Che Guevara, rolled up his sleeves with the working people in China, but he also really enjoyed engaging with the ancient Chinese literary luminaries and spent many a year translating old Chinese texts and poetry into English. Rewi wrote over 60 books about his experience of China as well as publishing his own poetry. In 1972, he was conferred an honorary doctorate of literature by Victoria University in Wellington.

In his eighties he and other gung-ho veterans revived the organisation and Rewi started thinking about revitalising the Shandan School so that it would meet the new challenges of the region. It reopened on the sixtieth anniversary of his arrival in China.

Rewi Alley's life's work and achievement as one of China's 'best-known and best-loved foreigners' has been immortalised in many ways; in a documentary film narrated by Sir David Lange; a portrait hanging in Beijing's national gallery; in an acclaimed opera performed—appropriately—by New Zealand and Chinese artists; in a University of Waikato prize for modern Chinese studies; on a plaque at his old school, Christchurch Boys' High; and in ten-yearly banquets held at the Great Hall of the People in Beijing to mark the decades since his birth.

Rewi Alley died in his adopted homeland 60 years after his arrival; he remains the only foreigner ever to be given a state funeral in China and a great tomb was erected in Shandan to house Alley's remains. If you ever travel that Old Silk Road, be sure to stop by and see the effect one Kiwi and the phrase 'gung-ho' had on China.

# NIGEL RICHARDS 1967–

*First two-time Scrabble world champion*

*First on the tiles*

The first Kiwi to be world-champion Scrabble player was former Christchurch City Council water department worker, Nigel Richards, who attained his world champ status in 2007 when he was 40.

Sporting a bowl-cut, bushy-bearded Nigel took up competitive Scrabble playing in 1997, when he started to make his first-rate tile moves at the Christchurch Scrabble Club. In 2011, with his second world-championship win, Nigel set a new world record by being the first person ever to win two world championships, roundly beating an Australian opponent after numerous rounds and knockouts filled with mounting tension.

Over four days, players in the 2011 championship scored a collective total of 1,499,107 points in 1801 games, which equates to an average of 832 points per game—certainly a different kettle of fish to the friendly games played in homes around the world.

Competitive Scrabble players are a different breed to the casual player. They spend years honing their skill—memorising hundreds of two- and three-letter combinations that maximise on point scoring when placed strategically—and passing multiple qualifying rounds to secure entry into the championship.

In his winning 2007 match, Nigel got four bonus scores for getting all seven letters out—for dirtiest, overapt, recopies and equinias—worth 86 points and clinching the game.

Nigel, who now lives in Kuala Lumpur but plays as a New Zealand representative, is a nine-time winner of the King's Cup in Bangkok, the biggest Scrabble competition in the world, and three-time USA national Scrabble champion. The next world championships are to be held in October 2013—go Nigel! For another New Zealand plastic tile winner, see Tantrix, (page 152).

# KIWIFRUIT

*The tale of how one overworked and underpaid woman*
*was the first to bring a fruit to the Kiwis*

Isabel Fraser was born in Dunedin in 1863. She completed teacher training and got her BA from the University of Otago in 1887, and graduated MA with honours in physics two years later.

After a few years teaching around the country, in 1893, she was appointed headmistress at Wanganui Girls' College, where, under her stewardship, the school gained a reputation as a fine establishment for young ladies. Running New Zealand's largest boarding school for girls was no walk in the park, especially when Isabel had strong ideas about progressive education for girls—preferring to undertake practical as well as academic teaching. The all-male board of governors weren't her most empathetic supporters, and any loss that the school made was taken out of Isabel's wage (though she would not receive any of the profit, should the school make it). Isabel ran the everyday school duties, implemented many new initiatives such as physical education, swimming and the teaching of first-aid and resuscitation skills as well as encouraging staff to engage students in 'conversation learning' rather than rote-learning. She was also expected to teach daily classes.

This demanding job was entirely exhausting and, in June 1903, Isabel was granted leave of absence. Not one to sit around and stare out the window as she rested, Isabel sailed for Japan and stopped off in China for a spell to visit her sister Katie who was working at a mission in Yichang (a mountainous town that lies on the northern bank of the Yangtze River), and together they worked in mission schools.

Isabel returned to Whanganui in January 1904, bringing with her the small black seeds of a fruit she had enjoyed in Yichang. It was known to the locals as '*yang tao*' (variously described as 'monkey peach', 'strawberry peach', or 'sun peach'). Isabel stayed headmistress at the college until 1910 when she established Iona College in Hawke's Bay.

Isabel passed the seeds to a local orchardist, who then passed them to his brother who had an interest in exotic plants. Nurseryman Alexander Allison planted the seeds in 1906, which grew into big-leafed vines, and in 1910 the first fruit appeared. Unlike anything else grown in the country at the time, these brownish egg-shaped furry-skinned fruit with bright green flesh reminded some of the taste of gooseberries. They hailed from China, so became known as Chinese gooseberries.

In 1928, in the Bay of Plenty, Hayward Wright was responsible for the first New Zealand commercial kiwifruit orchard, cultivating a green kiwifruit variety (*Actinidia deliciosa*) he then named after himself. The Hayward cultivar is now the most common globally grown kiwifruit.

It takes up to seven years for the kiwifruit vine to produce fruit, so the fact that in the 1960s much of the dairy farms in Te Puke and surrounding area converted to kiwifruit orchards showed how willing the region was to take calculated risks to generate a profit from such an unknown exotic import soon-to-be-turned-export.

Kiwifruit thrives in the Bay of Plenty region with its fertile soils and warm climate, and an easy distance to the Port of Tauranga, and Te Puke proudly claims the title of kiwifruit capital of New Zealand. Should you be in the area, you can visit the giant kiwifruit at Te Puke.

Today, New Zealand's 2700 kiwifruit growers produce approximately 110 million trays or 400,000 tonnes of kiwifruit (93 per cent exported) from 13,350 hectares of orchard canopy area. Roots of mature kiwifruit vines grow to depths of up to 30 metres while each vine can support as many as 1500 fruit, and a vine planted in the 1930s is still productive 80 years later.

Until about 2008, all New Zealand commercial kiwifruit cultivars could be traced back to those original seeds collected as a curiosity on Isabel Fraser's OE.

## CHRISTINE COLE CATLEY 1922–2011

*First to put kiwi to fruit*

The woman who wrote the acclaimed biography of Beatrice Tinsley (see page 35) was also the first to incorporate the name of our iconic national bird into the name of our iconic fruit export.

New Zealand started exporting 'Chinese gooseberries' in significant quantities in the 1950s, and Eva Thompson was the first person to send cold-store kiwifruit overseas. However, the fruit, although delicious and able to travel, wasn't doing terribly well and was languishing on fruit store shelves in the United Kingdom and the United States. Something had to be done. Enter Christine Cole Catley.

In 1961, New Zealand fruit growers were trying to entice the American market to buy large quantities of this fruit which was doing really well in our orchards. Christine Cole Catley was working as an advertising copywriter and was charged with the rename and rebrand. Christine came up with the name 'Kiwi berry', which soon evolved into kiwifruit. (The Americans call the fruit kiwis, so whether they are termed berries or fruit is of no matter to them.)

Christine, who grew up in the Rangitikei town of Hunterville (see page 216), had a number of other firsts. When television came to Wellington, she was the first TV critic for the *Dominion*, writing under the nom de plume Sam Cree. In a humorous twist, at the same time she wrote television reviews for the *Dominion*'s sister paper, the *Sunday Times*, but under the nom de plume Hillary Court. Sometimes the two reviewers' opinions would clash. Christine thought this was, 'naughty but great fun'.

Cole Catley was appointed to the New Zealand Broadcasting Council—'We set up TV1 and TV2 to compete in excellence. How innocent we were'—but was dismissed by Robert Muldoon as they didn't see eye to eye.

For seven years in the 1960s, Christine headed New Zealand's first full-time journalism course at Wellington Polytechnic's School of Journalism, and demanded that half the students were female. This insistence consequently vastly increased the number of women employed in the media and redressed the masculine bias of the media's collective voice; many of her former students—including 'mother of the nation' Judy Bailey—went on to attain key positions within the industry.

As a writer, editor and publisher (establishing her own publishing company in the 1970s), Christine Cole Catley had many literary connections and was always working to foster and mentor literary endeavours: she was the chair of the Frank Sargeson Literary Trust, and initiated the Michael King Writers' Centre in Devonport. In 2006, she was made a Distinguished CNZM. When Christine died in 2011 her autobiography covering her 88 years was near completion. She claimed that her work with the New Zealand Parents Centre was her greatest achievement.

In 1945—a conservative era in New Zealand—Christine was openly a solo mother, and in 1952 she co-founded the Parents Centre New Zealand, which focused on the importance of mother and child bonding, increasing awareness of the emotional aspects of childbirth and encouraging fathers to attend births.

## FIRST ON THE BOX

New Zealand was a bit of a late bloomer in the realm of television. At 7.30 p.m. on Wednesday 1 June 1960 Auckland had the nation's first encounter with broadcast pictures—three hours of programming was transmitted from the New Zealand Broadcasting Corporation's 1YA radio broadcasting facility at 74 Shortland Street in Auckland, now home to the University of Auckland's Gus Fisher Gallery. It took another two years for televised broadcasts to reach Wellington and the South Island.

# HAROLD WILLIAMS 1876–1928

### First Kiwi in charge of The Times

Around the world, up to 7000 different languages are estimated to be spoken. Some people are content to know just one language, and many are bilingual. If you speak two or more languages you are considered a polyglot, and if you speak six or more languages, you are a hyperpolyglot.

Harold Williams—the first New Zealander to be a foreign editor of *The Times*—knew 58 languages and dialects and was one of the world's greatest linguists.

Harold, born in Auckland in 1876, was the eldest of seven children. At the age of seven he had what he termed 'an explosion in his brain', and from then until he started high school (Timaru and Christchurch boys' high schools) he taught himself Latin, Greek, Hebrew, French, German, Spanish, Italian, Maori, Samoan, Tongan, Fijian and had pieced together the vocabulary of the Dobuan language spoken in New Guinea. His hunger for languages was fed by visiting the Auckland dockyards and speaking with Polynesian and Melanesian crews. Despite his obvious skill at language acquisition—discerning vocabulary rules and patterns—Harold was miserable at mathematics and because of this, he was unable to achieve a BA degree.

His father urged him to join the Methodist ministry, which enabled Harold to visit various communities and absorb their languages, including the Dalmatian population near Dargaville. His northern exploits coincided with and simultaneously spurred on his reading of Leo Tolstoy's works and Harold took on some of the values of his literary hero, becoming a vegetarian, pacifist and socialist. He then headed off to explore the world and further satisfy his hunger for languages.

In 1900 he left New Zealand studying philology, ethnology, philosophy, history and literature at Munich University, teaching English part-time and earning his PhD—appropriately—in languages in 1903.

Moving to Russia, he met his literary hero Tolstoy in 1905. Tolstoy reportedly asked Harold why he had learnt Russian and was bemused to hear Williams reply, 'Because I wanted to read *Anna Karenina* in the original.'

The gruff Tolstoy responded, 'But how many languages do you know?' And then insisted that Williams list all his languages.

At the time, he knew at least 50, including Zulu, Swahili and Hausa. Tolstoy could not help but be impressed. He wasn't the only one; Harold Williams earned the respect of many thinkers of the day, including HG Wells.

Harold reported back to the western world the events of the Bolshevik revolution as they unfolded. In 1922, he was appointed foreign editor of *The Times* and was responsible for interpreting and commenting on international political events at a time of immense change and complexity.

# 5

# FIRST PEOPLES AND FIRST STEPS

## ALLAN WILSON 1934–91

*Evolutionary revolutionary*

*First to understand evolution at a molecular level and
bring human evolution forward 20 million years*

*First to shed light on the age of the Origin of the Species*

Ask anyone who the lead thinker in the field of evolution is, and 95 per cent of people will say Charles Darwin. New Zealanders should start to challenge that, because one of the most important theorists of evolutionary change—and certainly someone more contemporary—was Allan Wilson who was born in Ngaruawahia in 1934.

Although brought up on the back blocks of dairy country, this quiet and unassuming Kiwi made the scientific world turn somersaults when

95

he applied the molecular clock to human evolution and suggested his Out of Africa theory.

As a small lad, Allan had been fond of asking a great many questions regarding the Bible stories he was told at Sunday school. His astute questioning impressed the vicar's wife who then encouraged his family to enrol Allan at King's College in Auckland.

While attending high school in the late 1940s, Allan wasn't taught evolutionary science, he happened upon it one evening when sheltering in the library after missing his train and waiting for another.

From the moment he opened that first book, Allan became fixated on the science of evolution. Thinking that his future would somehow combine farming with scientific advances, Allan enrolled at the University of Otago—the first in his family to undertake tertiary education.

Unusually for the times, Allan had an interest in both zoology and biochemistry, so he received his BSc in zoology and chemistry and was then invited by a visiting US zoology lecturer to study at Washington State University. Here he completed an MA and declared in a typically sanguine manner that he would solve the problem of evolution. He chose Berkley for his PhD in biochemistry because he was determined to investigate evolution from a biochemical perspective, rather than the paleontological perspective with which it had been investigated since Darwin's days. He stayed at Berkley for 35 years, with a 26-year tenure as a member of the faculty, and attracted a large group of students and research associates.

Allan became fascinated with the relationships between divergent species of birds and spent much time hanging out at Berkley's Museum of Vertebrate Zoology which housed a huge collection of bird specimens.

Darwin's theory of natural selection—a natural mechanism where the fittest members of a species survive to pass on their genetic information, while the weakest die off because they are unable to compete—was accepted as the one and only evolutionary tenet. Using this model, it was speculated that the earliest humans split from their ape-like ancestors around 25 million years ago.

However, Allan Wilson decided there was more to the science of evolution than comparing fossilised remains; he wanted to find a quantitative answer as to how birds and humans had evolved—he found it at a molecular level.

Allan studied the changes of protein in examples of divergent species over time. In 1967 in a paper published in *Science*, he showed that apes and humans are much more closely related—diverging only 5–6 million years ago.

Over millions of years, mutations in protein accumulate steadily; in measuring the number of changes in blood proteins between two divergent species, Allan realised he could read the data as historical documents, and therefore calculate how long it had been since those species shared a common ancestor.

Allan, with his research collaborator, anthropologist Vince Sarich, coined the phrase 'molecular clock' and compared the proteins of chimpanzees and humans and found that they are very similar; by counting back the number of changes between humans and chimps, the molecular clock showed that we shared a common ancestor 20 million years later than what had been thought originally.

This new outlook on the question of human evolution was hugely controversial at the time—many academics slammed it as absurd. Scientists had looked at evolution from evidence of the fossilised past—now Allan Wilson was effectively using the present to look back at the past and this relationship between time and genetic change cast a whole new light on the theory of evolution.

It took decades for Allan's revolutionary evolutionary theory to be accepted as fact—and by the time advances in biochemistry, genetics and molecular biology had proven him correct, Allan dropped another theoretical bombshell on the scientific world.

In 1987, with collaborators Rebecca Cann and Mark Stoneking, and with the advancement in understanding how DNA works (thanks in part to Maurice Wilkins, see page 42), Allan used emerging molecular technology to find a genetic mother for human kind.

By looking at DNA passed on directly from mother to child (mito-chondrial DNA), Allan announced in his paper that all modern humans derived from a 'Mitochondrial Eve' who lived in Africa around 150,000 years ago. This Out of Africa theory that said humans effectively had the same racial genetic make-up was in complete contrast to the widespread belief that modern humans had simultaneously evolved on different continents, with different races having different ancient ancestors.

Again Allan Wilson received a great deal of criticism, especially from religious groups who read into his findings that Eve was black. But again his revolutionary theory has been accepted and led to many further discoveries, and his scientific thought still underpins the work of evolutionary biologists worldwide.

He was elected to the Royal Society of London, to the American Academy of Arts and Sciences and was awarded the 3M Life Sciences Award and is the only New Zealander thus far to receive the MacArthur Prize (dubbed the 'Genius' award). Allan Wilson was diagnosed with leukaemia in 1990 and died on 21 July 1991 at the age of 56, while undergoing treatment for the disease and when his Eve theory was still causing controversy.

Allan Wilson asked the right questions, and in doing so he shook the foundation of what humans thought we knew about our evolution. His work confirmed Darwin's theories that all species were related and had common ancestors and that humans evolved relatively recently from a common ape ancestor in Africa.

Despite the debate surrounding his work, Allan was well respected and trained more than 200 graduate students and future evolutionary scientists at his Berkley laboratory. Allan's revolutionary work—now thought of as completely mainstream—is taught in high schools world-wide, and a research centre has been set up under his name. The

Allan Wilson Centre for Molecular Ecology and Evolution, based at Massey University, carries on this great Kiwi scientist's work, advancing knowledge of the evolution and ecology of New Zealand and Pacific plant and animal life, and human history in the Pacific.

Although Darwin's theory of evolution is held alongside Allan Wilson's microbiological theory as a tenet of evolutionary theory, we can say that Darwin was very wrong about one thing. When he visited the Bay of Islands for nine days in 1835, Darwin wasn't that impressed by our extraordinarily unique range of flora and fauna which had evolved after millions of years in isolation, from the tuatara—who watched dinosaurs evolve and then die, to giant carnivorous snails and the captivating flightless kakapo. Darwin branded New Zealand as 'not a pleasant place'. We all know that to be untrue.

## THE FIRST WHITE SETTLERS TO LIVE IN NEW ZEALAND

In the late eighteenth century, New Zealand's dense forests of towering trees were found to be ideal for repairing whaling ships and also for escaping into. In 1799, while the crew from the ship *Hunter*, anchored in the Firth of Thames, were gathering timber, Thomas Taylor and three other seamen deserted and made a home with local Maori. These four men—possibly all escaped convicts—could be called the first Pakeha-Maori. Taylor married a local woman and met the crews of two ships that arrived in the Firth of

Thames in 1801, acting as an interpreter for one vessel that ran aground and was in need of food supplies and help to refloat the vessel. Taylor also gave details to one of the ships' captains about Maori life. His further activities, and the fate of his fellow deserters, is unknown.

By the early nineteenth century, the kahikatea and pohutukawa trees that the timber merchants had been felling were deemed to be unsuitable for ship building. Ships were less frequent visitors to the Firth, and deserters were more able to start anew.

In 1804, convict sailor James Cavanagh took the opportunity to escape the New South Wales government vessel *Lady Nelson,* and fled into the bush off the Cavalli Islands on Northland's east coast—very near the place that the *Rainbow Warrior* wreck is now serving as a dive destination and marine-life sanctuary. Cavanagh lived with local Maori and avoided further European contact.

The story of two of the first European females to arrive in Aotearoa is somewhat more scandalous and intriguing.

## CHARLOTTE BADGER 1778–1807

*New Zealand's first European female settler was
a felon and a pirate and a solo mum*

Baptised in Bromsgrove, Worcester, England, on 31 July 1778, Charlotte Badger was brought before the court when she was eighteen years old, convicted of breaking and entering; the spoils of her crime—a silk handkerchief and a couple of guineas—were taken from her. Charlotte's crime was deemed a capital felony and she was sentenced to seven years' transportation.

In 1801, five years after sentencing (and spending the waiting years in confinement), and after a gruelling 206-day voyage, Charlotte arrived at Port Jackson (Sydney) and started her incarceration at the pleasantly named Parramatta Female Factory. While there she made friends with Catherine Hegarty. Five years after her arrival at the prison, Charlotte became pregnant (we can assume that there were a few males around the female factory), and gave birth to a daughter.

Charlotte, her child and Catherine were selected to be shipped aboard the *Venus* to Hobart where they would finish the last two years of their sentence as servants for new settlers. The ship's captain had found himself short-staffed, so had taken on a few male convicts to help with the sailing of the cargo of flour, grain and salt pork. It seems from allegations by the captain, however, that the motley crew were interested in finding out about each other and getting to grips with the contents of the barrels of whisky on board the *Venus* rather than sailing.

On the north coast of Tasmania, on a stopover in Twofold Bay, Port Dalrymple, the captain disembarked to deliver some official dispatches and the convicts grabbed this opportunity to mutiny, and seized control of the ship, putting ashore the crew members loyal to the captain. Captain

Chase must have been quite disgruntled when he saw his ship and full cargo sail away into the wild blue yonder.

A notice in the *Sydney Gazette* in July 1806 read:

WANTED FOR PIRACY
Whereas the persons undermentioned and described, did, on the 16th day of June, by force and arms violently and piratically take away from His Majesty's settlement of Port Dalrymple, a Colonial Brig or Vessel called 'VENUS . . . etc . . . Description of same: CHARLOTTE BADGER age 23yrs, convict, very corpulent, full face, thick lips, with infant child.' CATHERINE HAGERTY, middle sized, light hair, fresh complexion, much inclined to smile. BENJAMIN KELLY, thin faced, small build, etc . . .

Although Charlotte's story is more documented, it seems that Catherine may have had the natural resources to spark the whole piratical episode. Some accounts have Catherine and Charlotte as the instigators of the adventure, and some state that although they weren't the ringleaders, they were encouraging accomplices. The mutineers were aided by the ship's first mate, Benjamin Kelly, who seemed to be a bit beguiled by Catherine Hegarty's fair face and winsome smile and they were to cohabit for their journey to unknown shores. Charlotte and fellow convict John Lancashire apparently also shared quarters; the good ship *Venus*—an olden-day Love Boat—set course for the Bay of Islands, New Zealand.

When the *Venus* pitched up at Rangihoua the two couples disembarked and set up a new life alongside the Nga Puhi. The *Venus* continued its voyage down the coastline, and its remaining convict crew, unable to navigate and proving to be ever more villainous and piratical—kidnapping and enslaving Maori women—found their karma when their ship came into distress along the Coromandel Peninsula and local Maori took the opportunity to seize and burn it for the scrap iron on board. It is quite possible that the convict-pirates ended up being eaten in revenge for their plundering lifestyle.

So it was that Charlotte Badger, her daughter and Catherine Hegarty were the first recorded European females to settle in New Zealand, although Catherine is said to have succumbed to disease and died in April 1807. Benjamin Kelly and John Lancashire apparently upped sticks, too, and were recaptured and returned to London to live out their sentence.

Charlotte Badger supposedly lived with a Nga Puhi chief and refused all offers of passage back to European society; although one account claims she eventually sailed off to America with a whaling captain ten years later, there is no definitive evidence and her story ends here. She wasn't mentioned in Samuel Marsden's accounts of new life in the Bay of Islands in 1814.

Historical novels have been written about Charlotte Badger and even a stage musical was produced and shown in Charlotte's hometown of Bromsgrove (film rights are apparently still up for option, if any one is interested). A gun of the type that might have been used in the mutiny is held at Te Papa Museum in Wellington.

Australia claims Charlotte and Catherine as their first female pirates, but in fleeing Australia, perhaps the female buccaneers would be happier being claimed by New Zealand.

## ARTHUR LESLIE LYDIARD 1917–2004

*The first to just do it—(jogging)*

Thanks to Hollywood, half the world probably believes that Forrest Gump taught them how to run and improve their general fitness. However, we Kiwis know that it is running guru Arthur Lydiard who was responsible for bringing regular fitness practice—and, indirectly, running shoes—to the world stage.

Arthur is the man who brought jogging to the fore (but we won't blame him for Lycra and short shorts) and, worldwide, millions of people have benefited from his systematic approach to physical fitness. But how did he get there?

Born in Auckland in 1917, Arthur Lydiard attended Mount Albert Grammar School and enjoyed rugby, swimming and cycling. After leaving school, he began an apprenticeship with a shoe factory, and learnt the craft, staying there for 24 years. He was active in his twenties, but when, one day, the then 27-year-old Lydiard struggled to keep pace with an older friend on an 8-kilometre run, he realised he needed to start a fitness regime in order to keep the slowing effects of age at bay.

Despite this photographic evidence, Lydiard was not responsible for short shorts. He was, however, responsible for bringing jogging to the world

After the Second World War, it was the fashion to push on through pain at all costs. The adage of 'no pain, no gain' was at its height of popularity, and those interested in athletics would push themselves to their limits—running short distances at high speeds, but not building up a base-level fitness. Arthur tried this training out, but soon realised he needed to develop his own personal programme.

He read up on fitness, and started to train daily. Lydiard was soon clocking up the miles, running hundreds of kilometres a week and alternating difficult and easy efforts. He started to find that with a combination of stamina-building distance runs and finessing fast sprints, he could build top strength and speed.

His well thought out theories were, in essence, the philosophy of jogging:

> ... long, even-pace running at a strong speed produced increased strength and endurance—even when it is continued to the point of collapse—and was beneficial, not harmful, to regular competition.

While many professional runners would retire as they edged nearer to their thirties, Arthur Lydiard took up competitive running, lost weight, gained fitness and realised—as many modern runners now do—that he was addicted to the long hard slog.

The changes in physique, strength and overall fitness were obvious, and others interested in achieving the same started training with Lydiard who would run up and over a 35-kilometre course in Auckland's Waitakere Ranges. His fitness conditioning advice was sought by numerous people and Arthur became a coach. In his mid-thirties, Lydiard won the national marathon title in 1953 and 1955 before retiring from competition and concentrating on coaching.

The group of runners being mentored by Arthur included some of the greatest of all New Zealand track athletes: Barry Magee, Murray Halberg, and Peter Snell. These runners were not an official team, but a bunch of Aucklanders who enjoyed running together and improving their personal strength and fitness.

Lo and behold, on a sweltering summer's day in Rome a few years later, Peter Snell and Murray Halberg (800 metres and 5000 metres, respectively) won gold medals within an hour of each other at the 1960 Olympics. A few days later, Barry Magee aced a bronze medal in a world-best marathon.

At a time when Eastern-bloc Olympic teams were meticulously handpicking their athletic talent using 'scientific' and genetic analysis, Lydiard had taken the raw talent of local lads and spurred them on to become world champions. He advocated that 'champions are everywhere you just have to train them correctly'.

It was the start of a golden era of New Zealand middle-distance and distance running, and the sports officials who had declined Arthur Lydiard an official team coaching position for the Olympics must've felt a little silly. Thankfully, the New Zealand public had seen Lydiard's talent for bringing out the championship potential of others and fundraised to get him there as an 'independently travelling unofficial coach'. Lydiard came home a public figure and national hero and was awarded an OBE in 1962.

At the 1964 Olympics, Arthur Lydiard was trackside as the official coach of the New Zealand athletics team, and Peter Snell won another gold medal.

Meanwhile Lydiard had kept working in the shoe industry and had even developed a sole that was more lightweight for running. Later he worked on a system of lacing that prevented the foot straining against the restrictive points of a shoe. He looked at all the details of running, including nutrition, and became the world's most respected athletics coach. Not only was he asked to mentor the Finnish, Mexican, Venezuelan, Turkish, Danish and Australian track teams, but he also became a highly respected motivational speaker in New Zealand. After one public address to a group of paunchy businessmen, many claimed that it was all very well for sporty young things to take up running, but their doctors—fearing coronary collapse—had emphatically told them to avoid exercise.

Arthur rubbished this medical logic, maintaining that light jogging for health was a better way for the heart to oxygenate, recuperate and build on itself after coronary attack. Running was also a lifesaver, and physically exerting yourself was far more beneficial than the bed rest as the proverbial ambulance at the bottom of a cliff.

In 1962 a guinea-pig group of twenty Auckland businessmen formed the Auckland Joggers Club. It was the world's first such club, but very few of the members could initially run 100 metres at a stretch. Eight months later, with the help of Lydiard's champion-building theories, eight of them ran marathons. This was true testament to the Lydiard approach, but the idea was yet to be taken on at a global scale.

Enter Bill Bowerman who was later to become co-founder of Nike. Bowerman was the coach of the University of Oregon relay team who Lydiard invited to New Zealand to match race with his team. Bowerman recalled how he was to first recognise the wisdom of the middle-distance guru:

The first Sunday I was down there, Lydiard asked me if I wanted to go out for a run with a local jogging club. I was used to going out and walking 55 yards, jogging 55 yards, going about a quarter of a mile and figuring I had done quite a bit . . . We went out and met a couple hundred people in a park—men, women, children, all ages and sizes. I was still full of breakfast as Lydiard pointed toward a hill in the distance and said we were going to run to Two Pine Knoll. It looked about 1 1/2 miles away. We took off and I wasn't too bad for about 1/2 mile, and then we started up this hill. God, the only thing that kept me alive was the hope that I'd die. I moved right to the back of the group and an old fellow, I suppose he was around 70 years old, moved back with me and said, 'I see you're having trouble.' I didn't say anything—because I couldn't. So we took off down the hill and got back about the same time the people did who had covered the whole distance.

—Bill Dellenger, *The Running Experience*

The two men shared training techniques and Lydiard was later to remark that he taught the American to make shoes, but Lydiard's impact on Bowerman was also physically evident. Bowerman spent six weeks with Lydiard, learning to jog slowly and comfortably and he returned to Oregon minus 10 pounds and having lost 4 inches from his waistline. Lydiard referred to an easy day's training as a 'jog'.

On his return to the USA, 50-year-old Bowerman started up his own Sunday morning club, and imported Lydiard's concept of jogging for which he later received a medal from President Kennedy. In receiving the honour, Bowerman said, 'I am but the disciple. Arthur Lydiard from

New Zealand is the prophet.' The running craze thus spread throughout America and the world; now millions of people pound the pavements, open roads, dirt tracks, beaches and grass fields, venturing up hill and down dale because of one Kiwi.

In 1965, Lydiard's book *Run for Your Life—Jogging with Arthur Lydiard* was published. The East Germans were so impressed by Lydiard's systematic and logical philosophy that they established a nationwide health and fitness programme called Run for Your Life. In six months, sports club membership in East Germany had doubled.

Also the same year—but apparently unrelated—the Beatles released their album *Rubber Soul*, containing the song 'Run for Your Life' which John Lennon later described as his least favourite Beatles track, but was George Harrison's favourite song on that album. Although this nice coincidence in history may be an unsubstantiated connection, it is rather nice to think that even the Fab Four were affected by Lydiard's credo.

Arthur Lydiard died in 2004, at the age of 87, while on tour in the USA. Lydiard's success and influence on fitness training is unparalleled.

His legacy lives on, with the West Auckland Legend marathon, held annually in September, following Lydiard's famous training route over the Waitakere Ranges. The Lydiard Foundation was co-established by Lorraine Moller, New Zealand 1992 Olympic women's marathon bronze medallist, to promote Lydiard's training philosophy. While nowadays, most coaches do not advocate clocking up the long distances for their high-performance athletes, many of the African athletes who dominated the first podiums at track events during the first years of the twenty-first century were basically trained on Lydiard's principles.

And by the way, Hollywood, Forrest Gump's fictional run across America and back again was set in 1977—two decades after a New Zealander started to invent jogging and the way that people got fit.

## THE FIRST NEW ZEALAND MILE UNDER FOUR MINUTES

Born in Eketahuna, Murray Halberg played rugby in his youth, but severely injured himself in a game, leaving his left arm crippled. He took up running in an effort not to waste his physical strength, and soon fell in step with Arthur Lydiard, who became his coach. At the 1958 British Empire and Commonwealth Games, Halberg, with Lydiard's training, became the first sub-four-minute miler from New Zealand.

Peter Snell's achievement of running a mile in 3 minutes, 54.4 seconds (on a grass track, no less) is immortalised with a life-sized statue in Whanganui's Cooks Gardens; Snell is mid-sprint, looking towards the finish line.

# SIR PETER BUCK TE RANGI HIROA 1877–1951

*First Maori medical doctor*

*Anthropologist of worldwide repute who helped the world understand the Maori and Pacific cultures and (probably) first New Zealander to receive a Swedish knighthood—Royal Order of the Pole Star*

Born in Urenui, Peter Henry Buck regarded his Maori and Pakeha ancestry as equally important and influential on his success in life. His mother and his great aunt instilled in him a high regard for Maori lore and language, and shared the oral history of his Ngati Mutunga ancestry. Peter inherited a love of language and poetry from his Irish-born father, who'd come to New Zealand via the Australian goldfields.

In later life Peter was given the name of a notable ancestor Te Rangi Hiroa by his elders, and he used it as a pen-name on his academic publications.

Peter went to the local state primary school and then attended Te Aute College, the Anglican secondary school for Maori boys in Hawke's Bay. There he learnt Latin and Greek, captained the first fifteen and the athletics team, was dux, passed his medical preliminary examination, and received a scholarship to study at the University of Otago medical school.

Other than being diligent in his university studies and one of the top students in his classes, he also showed prowess in athletics and in 1900 and 1903 was the national long jump champion. Buck also participated

Sir Peter Henry Buck signing an autograph book for
an unidentified girl at Marae, Ngarauwahia, Waikato

in the odd Otago jape—definitely more sophisticated than the scarfie
couch burners, students back then knew how to have a laugh; Peter
was involved in a mock hunt for a stuffed moa that had been 'captured'
from the museum.

Buck was house surgeon at Dunedin Hospital and worked part-time
at Sunnyside Mental Hospital—thus becoming the first Maori medical
doctor in 1904.

In 1905—the year he married Irish-born Margaret Wilson—he was
appointed as a medical officer to the northern Maori and he became

involved in a concerted campaign to improve the sanitation of Maori settlements and the health of the people. Margaret was very supportive of his career and encouraged him to push further in his professional life. Peter started to get a reputation as a thorough worker with sound diplomacy skills and an ease and ability to share the message of the benefits of better and consistent sanitation. With his knowledge of tikanga Maori (tradition and protocol), he was nominated by Maori leaders to stand as an MP for the Northern Maori and was elected to Parliament.

In 1910, Peter Buck was awarded his MD after writing a thesis on 'Medicine amongst the Maoris in ancient and modern times'. His thesis investigated the effect of negative or depressed and despondent emotions on personal health, and he outlined the adverse impact of a depressed psyche on the body's physical immunity—quite a modern insight for the times.

Interested in the origins, migrations and culture of Polynesian peoples of the Pacific, during the parliamentary recess, he travelled to Rarotonga and Niue on working holidays as a medical officer.

In February 1915, Buck was sent to Gallipoli with the Maori Volunteer contingent as medical officer. A fifth of the men were killed or wounded.

He said of the time:

Gallipoli was a dirty campaign . . . The fact that the evacuation pier was within range of machine-guns and shell fire disorganised the routine for dealing with the wounded in the big attack. The ration of water prevented not only washing our faces and bodies but also the washing of clothes. As a result, everyone was infested with vermin . . . Owing to the lack of cooking facilities, there were no regular hot meals for the men. There were no canteens or picture shows to distract the men from ever-present death. There were no back areas behind shellfire where the men could rest in safety . . .

Buck transferred to combat duty, became second-in-command of the New Zealand Pioneer Battalion sent to France and in 1918 he was recognised with a Distinguished Service Order (DSO).

On his return to New Zealand, Buck became director of the Maori Hygiene Division, part of the newly created Department of Health, in 1921. He was especially concerned with the high Maori death rate in the influenza pandemic and again started a crusade to reduce the spread of infectious diseases by improving sanitation. He worked with Maori community leaders, nurses and medical officers, and this and his warmth and easy persona helped promote his cause.

Having helped improve the mortality rates of the Maori people, Buck now invested his time and efforts in his love of anthropology—the study of human culture—accompanying professional anthropologists on field trips to record the music and culture of Maori communities.

He was particularly interested in the material culture—artefacts and tools used by a people—and published essays and articles, illustrated with his own line drawings. No longer an amateur, Buck established himself as the leading authority on Maori material culture, and his talks at lecture halls nationally and internationally drew much attention and respect for his empirical and pragmatic thinking.

He was offered a five-year research fellowship at the Bishop Museum in Hawaii and there he carried out extensive fieldwork in the Pacific, starting in Western Samoa and going in later years to most of the other Polynesian island groups. In 1932 he was appointed visiting professor of anthropology at Yale University, which gave him the opportunity to extensively travel within the United States and to Canada, Britain and Europe, where he examined and corrected mislabelling of museum collections of Pacific artefacts. He also dispelled the European theory of Polynesian races being naturally and predominantly promiscuous.

Buck became the director of the Bishop Museum in 1936 and his long list of awards and honorary doctorates go some way to establish to the modern reader how esteemed he was among his contemporaries: the Hector Memorial Medal and Prize (1932), the Rivers Memorial Medal (1936), S. Percy Smith Medal (1951), the Huxley Medal (1952, posthumously); honorary doctorates from the University of New Zealand (1937), Rochester University (1939), the University of Hawaii (1948), and Yale (1951). He received a New Zealand knighthood in 1946 and also that year he was awarded the Swedish Order of the North Star—an honour conferred on those who have achieved 'civic merits, for devotion to duty, for science, literary, learned and useful works and for new and beneficial institutions'.

His honorary doctorate from Yale University praised him as 'First among those who know the peoples and cultures of the Polynesian world, medical doctor, warrior, ethnologist, author and poet, you have brought many races of people to greater understanding and peace.'

Although Sir Peter Buck lived the rest of his years in Hawaii, his fondness for New Zealand, and extensive correspondence over the years with Sir Apirana Ngata, meant that he still kept updated with the political and cultural developments of his homeland. He'd previously tried to get an academic post, but universities were unable to offer a position in his chosen field, and the focus of academia at that time was looking backward towards Britain, rather than at the new roads into Polynesian research that Peter Buck was forging. Before his death in 1951, Buck made a final trip home, visiting marae in many parts of the country. His ashes were laid to rest near Urenui in 1954.

With career highlights as varied and impressive as national long jump champion, doctor, public administrator, military man, politician, anthropologist, and museum director, Sir Peter Buck Te Rangi Hiroa is certainly a Kiwi to be proud of.

Sir Peter Buck's bicultural upbringing was key to his success, but his Maori heritage had a prominent part to play on his path to becoming the foremost anthropologist of Maori and Polynesian peoples. Above his desk in Honolulu hung the waka paddle given to him by his great aunt, and in a letter back home he said of it:

> I have studied under learned professors in stately halls of learning, but as I look at that paddle I know that the teacher who laid the foundation of my understanding of my own people, and the Polynesian stock to which we belong, was a dear old lady with tattooed face in a humbled hut walled in with tree-fern slabs.

# GEORGINA BEYER 1957–

*The world's first transgender mayor and transsexual Member of Parliament*

In 1995 the small Wairarapa town of Carterton made a name for itself by electing the world's first transgender mayor, Georgina Beyer, who later became the world's first transsexual to be elected into Parliament in 1999. With a background in theatre (appearing on New Zealand television staples such as *Close to Home* and *Shortland Street*), Georgina Beyer deftly handled the politics game, serving as the Wairarapa MP for seven years, strengthening the region's healthcare facilities and passing the Prostitution Reform Act as well as the Civil Unions Act.

In her maiden parliamentary speech, Georgina acknowledged a few Kiwi firsts:

> Mr Speaker, I can't help but mention the number of firsts that are in this Parliament. Our first Rastafarian [Nándor Tánczos] . . . our first Polynesian

woman . . . and yes, I have to say it, I guess, I am the first transsexual in New Zealand to be standing in this House of Parliament. This is a first not only in New Zealand, ladies and gentlemen, but also in the world. This is an historic moment. We need to acknowledge that this country of ours leads the way in so many aspects. We have led the way for women getting the vote. We have led the way in the past, and I hope we will do so again in the future in social policy and certainly in human rights.

# JOHN MONEY 1921–2006

*First to definitively explain how we account for our gender*

Although often controversial, Morrinsville-born Dr John Money was one of the world's leading authorities on gender identity and gender reassignment surgery. Money was a Harvard-educated author of many books, including *Gay, Straight, and In-Between: The Sexology of Erotic Orientation* (1988). As an expert on sexual behaviour, Money suggested that gender was learned rather than innate. He coined the term 'gender role' which can be described as the demonstrable actions (things we may say or do) that give others a basis for figuring out if we are male, female, or neither of those categories.

**6**

# EITHER ELEMENTAL OR PLASTIC

## ERNEST RUTHERFORD 1871–1937

*First tickled the nucleus into revealing its secrets*

*First New Zealand scientist to win a Nobel Prize*

*The world's 'first successful alchemist'*

Ernest Rutherford is one of the most illustrious scientists of all time. He is to the atom what Darwin is to evolution, Newton to mechanics, Faraday to electricity and Einstein to relativity. His pathway from rural child to immortality is a fascinating one . . .

—Dr John A Campbell, *Rutherford: Scientist Supreme*

It is given to but few men to achieve immortality, still less to achieve Olympian rank, during their own lifetime. Lord Rutherford achieved both. In a generation that witnessed one of the greatest revolutions in the entire history of science he was universally acknowledged as the leading explorer of the vast infinitely complex universe within the atom, a universe that he was first to penetrate.

—*New York Times* 1937 Eulogy

Einstein called him 'a second Newton', his students nicknamed him 'The Crocodile', and his family called him 'Ern', but we'll call him New Zealand's first Nobel Prize winner and one of the world's greatest scientists of all time (so far).

Have you ever counted the seconds between a lightning flash and a crack of thunder to work out if a storm is moving closer or further away?

Have you ever wondered how smoke detectors work?

Have you ever contemplated what exactly stuff is made of?

Ever considered how old Earth is?

Ever used wireless technology?

If it wasn't for Ernest Rutherford we'd still be wondering how these things work.

Ernest Rutherford was born in Brightwater, Nelson, the fourth of twelve children in a family where money was scarce, but enthusiasm towards education was not. His father was a mechanic, engineer and flax miller, while his mother—a former teacher—strongly held to the idea that knowledge was power and that, 'We haven't the money, so we've got to think.'

At primary school, Ernest was a bit of a loner and was given the disparaging nickname of 'Dopey'. It's a lovely paradox that his biographer,

Not so dopey, Sir! Ernest Rutherford (right) in the physics laboratory of Manchester University with Hans Geiger

Dr John Campbell, lists as his research interests: defect modes in doped crystals—though most people may be a touch too dopey to know what doped crystals are, in which case, Doctor Campbell would be the person to contact.

At the age of ten, Ernest was given his first book on science, and from there he adapted an experiment used to estimate the distance of an (imaginary) enemy's fired canon to measure the distance of a thunderstorm.

Obviously bright and forever querying the world around him, young Ernest was encouraged in his studies. He was head boy and dux at Nelson College, but was also a good New Zealand schoolboy and played forward in the school's first fifteen team and participated in the boxing ring. But his achievements didn't come easy or the first time round.

An interesting aspect about Ernest Rutherford's life is it seems to be a prime example of that tenet of 'if at first you don't succeed, try and try again'—Rutherford was often stumped when working on his experiments and theories, but with determination and diligence and thinking around a problem, he would attain success. This pattern of first failure and then success was evident from his primary school years, when, as times were hard and only one in fifty primary school children could afford to go on to secondary education, he had to sit an exam for a scholarship. He failed his first attempt, but then achieved the entrance grade on sitting the exams again. Years later, when sitting his University Entrance exams, he needed to place in the top ten of the whole nation in order to win a scholarship; on his first attempt Ernest came in at number 26. But he tried again, returning to high school in order to re-sit the exams which upon second sitting he secured the scholarship.

In 1889 he attended the University of New Zealand at Canterbury College, graduating in 1893 with an MA (with first class honours in maths and physics) and in 1894 he won a scholarship to attend Trinity College, Cambridge, as a research student of electromagnetic phenomena at the Cavendish Laboratory.

In New Zealand, Rutherford had established himself as an outstanding researcher and innovator working at the forefront of electrical technology. And at Cambridge, Rutherford happened to be the university's first non-Cambridge-graduate research student.

Rutherford had initially been interested in developing wireless waves as a method of signalling, in the hopes of solving the problem of a ship's inability to detect a lighthouse in fog. Rutherford created and refined an apparatus that could detect electromagnetic waves over a distance of several hundred metres. But his supervisor JJ Thomson diverted Rutherford's focus to the study of the electrical conduction of gases.

It was a time of scientific breakthroughs and, just after X-rays and radioactivity were discovered, Rutherford became interested in understanding the phenomenon of radioactivity itself. In 1898 he identified two distinct radioactive rays—alpha and beta rays.

The same year Rutherford accepted a professorship at McGill University in Montreal, Canada. The well-equipped laboratory was financed by a tobacco millionaire who considered smoking a disgusting habit. So it is only apt that it was here that Rutherford demonstrated the principle that went on to become the basis of the modern smoke detector. He also discovered a radioactive gas, later to be called radon.

Ernest Rutherford's three legendary discoveries shaped modern science, created nuclear physics and changed the way that we envisage the structure of the atom today.

Rutherford's first major discovery and the one that gained him—in 1908 at the age of 37—the Nobel Prize for Chemistry was for finding that atoms of heavy elements tend to decay, and that this spontaneous disintegration of atoms could be used to measure the age of Earth's minerals—heralding the 'carbon dating' technique.

Since the ancient Greeks, it was believed that atoms were locked and stationary; later he would prove that the Greeks were again wrong when he split the atom—the Greek atomos means 'indivisible' from ἀ- (a-, 'not') and τέμνω (temnō, 'I cut'). However, Ernest Rutherford turned that assumption and, later, nomenclature on its head and changed the nature of science (and science of nature) entirely when he proved that not only could atoms move, atoms could also naturally change structure (changing from heavy elements to slightly lighter elements).

Now, for the science bit I refer to a quote from Rutherford's Den—a resource in Canterbury which explains and enthuses about all things Rutherford.

> The science associated with the work for which Rutherford received the 1908 Nobel Prize is illustrated on every $NZ100 note. The gridded graph shows two curved lines, one curving down—the radioactive decay—and the other curving up—an activation curve. These correspond to the changing of one atom into a different atom with a decrease (radioactive decay) in the number of the 'parent' atom and an equivalent increase in the number of 'daughter' atoms. The scale on the bottom part of the grid is in days and the overall curve is recording the rate at which each of the different atoms is decreasing or increasing.

So, next time you hold a crisp hundy in your hand, you will know, and feel more powerful because of that knowledge—not simply for the currency soon to be burning a hole in your wallet. Rutherford's mum was right, knowledge is power.

With the McGill professorship, Rutherford was finally financially secure enough to marry his long-time fiancée Mary Georgina Newton (the daughter of Rutherford's landlady in Christchurch, whose mother was a prohibitionist and suffragette). Ernest and Mary were married in 1900 in Christchurch. Their only child, Eileen, was born in 1901 (the same year he was awarded a DSc from the University of New Zealand), and it was joked at the time that they would call her Ione—due to Ernest's fascination with ions.

While we hail Rutherford as one of the greatest physicists, his Nobel Prize was in chemistry by virtue of being a 'study on the chemical aspect of element transmutation and radioactive substance'. At the award ceremony banquet, Rutherford quipped that although he was now used to seeing changes of matter, the quickest change he knew of was when he turned from a physicist to a chemist in an instant.

Rutherford's second discovery in 1911 became the basis for how we conceive of the atom today: picture the atom as a tiny nucleus surrounded by orbiting electrons, like a solar-system model.

He was knighted in 1914, becoming Sir Ernest Rutherford and in the years of the First World War did a lot of work on acoustic methods of detecting submarines. Harking back to his childhood thunderstorm experiment, Rutherford and another scientist patented an apparatus for determining the direction of submarine sound. He also tried to persuade the United States Government to keep young scientists away from the trenches and instead retain them for research; unfortunately he was unsuccessful in this cause.

In 1917, Rutherford's third great achievement, the splitting of the atom, made him, as Dr John Campbell says, 'the world's first successful alchemist'—by converting nitrogen into oxygen. Rutherford poetically claimed that he had 'broken the machine and touched the ghost of matter'.

Continuing with the alchemist theme, it was said that Rutherford could turn a common person into a first-class talent. Returning to Cambridge as a director of Cavendish Laboratory, he was an inspiring leader and helped steer numerous future Nobel Prize winners towards their great achievements, including the discovery of neutrons in 1932—which Rutherford had theorised about in 1921.

The crocodilian term of endearment used by his students could either be inspired by the fact that crocodiles are unable to turn their head and must always look forward or for his reputation as being rather loud and blustery so you could hear him coming before you saw him—just like the crocodile in *Peter Pan*. Either way, an artist was commissioned to carve a crocodile on the exterior wall of the Mond building at Cambridge as an acknowledgement of Rutherford's tenacity—it's still there to this day.

In return visits to New Zealand, Rutherford was fittingly welcomed as a hero, speaking at packed lecture halls and awakening the nation's interest in science—under his suggestion the DSIR was first established.

From 1925 to 1930 he was the president of the Royal Society of London and was raised from Sir to Lord Rutherford of Nelson in the

British peerage system in 1931. Rutherford's chief recreations were golf and motoring.

Ernest Rutherford died in Cambridge on 19 October 1937. His ashes were buried in the nave of Westminster Abbey, just west of Sir Isaac Newton's tomb.

James Chadwick, one of those who Rutherford steered towards success and the discoverer of the neutron, stated that Rutherford possessed:

a volcanic energy and an intense enthusiasm—his most obvious characteristic—and an immense capacity for work … There is a stock phrase—'to throw light on a subject.' This is exactly what Rutherford did. To work with him was a continual joy and wonder. He seemed to know the answer before the experiment was made, and was ready to push on with irresistible urge to the next. He was indeed a pioneer—a word he often used—at his best in exploring an unknown country, pointing out the really important features and leaving the rest for others to survey at leisure.

—*Nobel Laureates and Twentieth-Century Physics*, Mauro Dardo, Cambridge University Press, 2004

Rutherford's childhood home in Nelson welcomes Rutherford-interested visitors, where, in a garden setting, the story of Rutherford's life and work is told through a series of display panels and sound stations. There is a small bronze statue of a child stepping out into the future.

Rutherford's Den is a multi-media education centre housed in the very rooms where Nobel Prize winner Ernest Rutherford studied, attended lectures and undertook his earliest experiments at Canterbury College—now the Arts Centre of Christchurch. The facility is at the time of writing closed for post-earthquake repair and refurbishment.

He is the only New Zealander to have an element—rutherfordium (symbol Rf and atomic number 104; a synthetic element it is also, appropriately, radioactive)—named in his honour. The mineral rutherfordine is also named after him.

## COLIN MURDOCH 1929–2008

*First to shoot wildlife with a tranquilliser*

*First to invent the disposable syringe*

Most Kiwis love the natural world and will know and thank British naturalist Sir David Attenborough for being the face and voice of wildlife documentaries for five decades, helping us get up-close and personal with hundreds of different species of wild beast. Well, David Attenborough has a lot to thank one very clever Kiwi inventor for. Without the innovative mind and problem-solving skills of Colin Murdoch, Sir David wouldn't have been able to crouch down next to a sedated polar bear or Bengal tiger and enthuse about their flesh-tearing teeth. Colin Murdoch, a South Canterbury pharmaceutical and veterinary chemist, invented—and perfected—the tranquilliser dart gun in 1959, allowing wildlife vets and carers to get controlled and safe time with the wildest of animals.

But before this innovation, Murdoch invented something far more significant to the everyday health and wellbeing of humankind. Every year, around the world, 16 billion disposable syringes are used, and we have Colin Murdoch to thank for that; and little thanks to the New Zealand health authorities of the time.

Dr Alexander Wood is given the credit for developing the glass syringe and hypodermic needle at the Royal College of Physicians of Edinburgh in 1850. It was a medical revolution, but despite the glass syringes being sterilised after each use, health workers still noticed a high rate of infection as pathogens were transferred from patient to patient.

The next advancement came in 1956 when the Timaru chemist, Colin, was working as a veterinarian and trying to develop a method of vaccination that eliminated the risk of infection. Murdoch realised that despite careful sterilisation, crystalline antibiotic deposits (like those on glasses that have been in the dishwasher many times) on the inside walls of the syringes made bacteria resistant. The solution was the use of disposable syringes made from a less expensive material than glass—the idea for the plastic syringe had been found.

Obviously excited about his invention, and aware of the widespread beneficial effects it would have worldwide, Murdoch presented his disposable syringe to the New Zealand Health Department. They were less than encouraging, stating that the plastic device was 'abstruse' and claiming that doctors and the general public would find plastic syringes 'too futuristic'. Against such scepticism, the development of this truly life-saving invention was delayed for a few years because of lack of funding.

Eventually, Colin scraped together enough money to get it patented (one of his 46 patented inventions). Murdoch made numerous improvements, and then the syringe was marketed globally by an Australian company—another example of Australians taking something 'Kiwi' and bringing it to world attention—a collective lesson we as a nation should learn is to back ourselves. Some of the key developments used to market in Murdoch's range of plastic syringes were that they could be prefilled with a specific quantity of medication and a syringe used to take blood would fill itself.

His work on the tranquilliser gun came when he was working with colleagues trying to monitor the health of the tahr population which had made a home in the mountains of New Zealand.

The sort of dedicated inventor who would work late nights at his kitchen table, Murdoch also invented the childproof bottle cap and the silent burglar alarm.

Colin Murdoch received very little attention and glory for his ingenious innovations that must've saved millions of lives and that many depend on everyday. Murdoch did not become rich, deciding not to sue companies that violated his patents. Satisfied instead that they were helping people, he said, 'Patents give you the right to sue; they don't give you the money to sue. It just costs too much'.

Colin Murdoch and his wife Marilyn had four children and thirteen grandchildren before he died in 2008 at the age of 79, having lived for seventeen years after cancer claimed one of his eyes.

He'd struggled at school, being dyslexic, and later in life he had to fight against unimaginative minds and bureaucracy, but his scientific mental dexterity and ability to think around problems made him one of the Kiwis who really has changed the world.

Colin Murdoch won three gold medals at the World Inventions Fair in Brussels in 1976, has been honoured by the New Zealand Design Council, and was included on *Time* magazine's list of the 100 most influential people of the South Pacific in 1999 (why not the world, we'll never know). In 2000 he was made a Member of the New Zealand Order of Merit (MNZM), and in 2007 Murdoch's tranquilliser gun was featured on a stamp as part of New Zealand Post's Clever Kiwis series.

We really should give more ticker-tape parades to inventors and speak of them with the same enthusiasm that David Attenborough does with the giants of the wild.

## ALAN MacDIARMID 1927–2007

*New Zealand's first naturist Nobel Prize winner, and third Nobel Laureate*

*First to discover plastic as a conductor of electricity*

Alan Graham MacDiarmid, New Zealand's third Nobel Laureate, was born in Masterton in 1927.

The Great Depression was to impact on his family's fortunes and also heavily influenced Alan's world view. His father lost his engineering job, and the family had to learn to become more self-reliant. While at primary school, Alan contributed to the family by helping deliver local milk in the early mornings and as a high-school student at Hutt Valley High he had a newspaper run.

> My mother and father set the stage for nurturing a warm, loving united, mutually supportive family who always pulled together and also helped others outside the family in need when necessary. Although we did not have too much food, my mother was always inviting other, less fortunate people to meals. On such occasions, my older brothers and sister would frequently remind me and my younger sister at meals not to ask for more food by saying to us out loud at the table, 'FHB,' which meant, 'Family Hold Back,' i.e., don't eat too much!
>
> The fact that we were closely knit taught us the important aspects of interpersonal relationships. Everyone expects 'the important things' in life such as birthday and Christmas presents, but it is the 'little unimportant' actions which actually are the real important things. These put the flesh on the skeleton of any relationship. Several hundred of these each week—the unimportant, the unexpected, the unnecessary, 'the little things', are the things that really count.

Alan's interest in chemistry was sparked by chancing upon his father's old chemistry textbooks; he recalled poring over the thin pages 'in complete confusion, but with burning curiosity'.

Alan left school and financed his part-time study at Victoria University by taking on a part-time job shovelling coal, washing dirty laboratory equipment, sweeping floors and preparing chemicals for demonstrations in the chemistry department.

In 1951 he received his degree with first-class honours in chemistry, and attained a Fulbright scholarship to work towards his PhD in inorganic chemistry at the University of Wisconsin.

While on a visit to Tokyo in the mid-1970s—before the development of laptops, cellphones or hand-held gaming devices—a chance conversation Alan had over a pot of green tea with Dr Hideki Shirakawa, a polymer chemist, was the inspiration for his investigations which were to lead to the development of plastic conductors.

Shirakawa mentioned a silly lab error brought on by a language mistranslation when a Korean graduate student mistakenly used 1000 times the requisite amount of catalyst for a chemical reaction. The result was a jelly-like plastic with an aluminium-like sheen. Since this new muddled material shimmered like a metal, MacDiarmid speculated that it might be able to conduct electricity like a metal, so he invited Shirakawa to join him and a physicist, Alan Heeger, at the University of Pennsylvania to find out.

Their investigation confirmed that this new polymer (a pimped-up version of polyacetylene) was a surprisingly high electrical conductor—with conductivity almost as good as copper.

Before this interdisciplinary study, plastics were considered strictly as electrical insulators, valued because they were incapable of allowing electrical charges to move.

MacDiarmid's team chose to ignore this long-held theory that plastic could not and would not conduct, and the basis of this new plastic-fantastic revolution was the observation and investigation of something that could have been dismissed as a mistake. MacDiarmid said:

> What is at the edge of scientific or social acceptability today is often commonplace tomorrow . . . Whether something is good or bad, hot or cold, black or white, there's so much in the eye of the beholder. The greatest limitation on social progress is the mind.

'Conducting polymers', 'electronic polymers' or 'synthetic metals' are all now in use in industry and technology and in our everyday lives: laptops, smartphones, solar cells, electrical displays, antistatic clothing, thermal sensors, drug release systems, printed circuit boards, rechargeable batteries, smart glass, flat-screen displays, and are very much a lead part in the development of nanotechnology.

But before MacDiarmid's study there were no immediate applications for this new technology. 'Conducting polymers were an answer waiting for the pertinent question, which had not yet been asked,' he said.

At the turn of the millennium, Alan MacDiarmid was awarded the Nobel Prize in chemistry conjointly with Alan Heeger and Hideki Shirakawa.

MacDiarmid was revered by the Late Sir Paul Callaghan as one of the two greatest scientists New Zealand has ever produced, the other being Rutherford—it is interesting to note that history has linked them together, albeit tenuously.

Only in New Zealand would there be a two-degrees-of-separation connection between the country's first Nobel Prize winner and the third. As a youngster, Alan's father, Archie, had shared a holiday with Ernest Rutherford's family. Archibald recalled being very impressed with Ernest, who had made 28 gallons (127 litres) of rhubarb wine. If there was still a bottle of that wine in a dusty shed somewhere, it would be worth quite a bit.

Oftentimes the world acknowledges Kiwi firsts before we do, but Victoria University recognised Alan's achievements with the award of an honorary doctorate in 1999.

In 2000, the Royal Society of New Zealand made him an honorary fellow and awarded him the Rutherford Medal. Audiences packed lecture halls to capacity when he did a speaking tour of New Zealand in 2001 and enthralled all with his erudite and engaging clarity and warmth, conveying a deep love of intellectual challenges. He became a member of the Order of New Zealand (ONZ) in 2002.

In 2001, a state-of-the-art nanotechnology research centre, the Alan G. MacDiarmid Institute, opened in China at Jilin University, and Alan was very involved in it, learning Chinese in order to participate more fully in the discussions, but also because he loved learning new things.

Fond of waterskiing, camping holidays and a bit of sun-worship (it could be said that MacDiarmid is the first openly naturist Nobel Prize-winning chemist), Alan was also extremely productive; even into his seventies he was spending up to twelve hours in the lab, and in his 60 years as a professional scientist he had published more than 600 papers and attained 25 patents. Yet he still listed his first chemistry job as lab boy at Victoria University on his CV.

In 2010, Victoria University of Wellington named a new science building after him—perhaps one day a current lab caretaker working in the MacDiarmid building will be another New Zealand science pioneer.

Although he spent much of his adult life in America, he loved his homeland and died in 2007 just before a planned return visit to New Zealand. Here's a few words from his press conference after winning the Nobel prize to remember Alan:

People always say to me, 'You have truly achieved, given where you came from.' But I was brought up in New Zealand doing a lot of mountaineering. When you do mountaineering, you don't ever look behind you at where you came from. You look at the mountains ahead of you . . . You can be the most brilliant scientist in all the world; put you on a desert island with the very best scientific equipment and the very best library and you'll do uninteresting research. You must have interaction. You must have discussion.

This award to Alan Heeger and to Hideki Shirakawa and me is recognition of the work that we have done—each of us individually and together.

We have been fortunate to have first-class students—undergraduate, graduate and post-doctoral—in our groups. And I always say research coming from a given group can never be better than the people carrying it out. The prize is recognition of their work.

# ARCHIBALD McINDOE 1900–60

*Saline-bath and plastic surgery pioneer*

*Community-assisted occupational rehabilitation pioneer and practitioner*

Archibald Hector McIndoe was born in Dunedin in 1900. His mother was an artist and singer, and it was always hoped that Archie would follow in his father's footsteps as an accomplished typographer and printer. However, Archie had other plans, graduating from Otago medical school in 1923 having been awarded the Junior Medicine Prize, the Senior Clinical Surgery Medal, a Bachelor of Medicine, and a Bachelor of Chemistry.

He wanted to be more than an ordinary doctor, and thanks to his ambition and quick intellect he secured a scholarship to the Mayo Clinic in Minnesota. Founded by brothers William and Charles Mayo, the clinic still has a reputation for producing some of the world's best surgeons. McIndoe attained an MSc in pathology in 1927 and the precision of his cutting and surgical sewing as well as his quick and accurate medical judgements won him the notice and respect of his fellow students and his professors.

He had an easy charm and was considered by the Mayo brothers to be one of their brightest medical graduates, and was soon to prove himself as an innovative surgeon.

McIndoe found that the liver had two blood supplies and theorised that while one supply could be shut down, the other could be kept open during liver surgery; with his supervisor's consent, McIndoe proceeded to experiment in this new technique, and this new technique became known as 'McIndoe's operation'.

After being lured by the offer of a professorship at London University which was then inexplicably denied by the English surgeon who had made the offer, Archie found himself at a loss for what to do in England, but a letter from his mother advised him of a relative, Harold Gillies (see page 146), who was a pre-eminent plastic surgeon. Harold became McIndoe's friend, mentor and partner, and two New Zealanders abroad became one of medicine's greatest partnerships.

Through Gillies, McIndoe secured a position at St Bartholomew's and then went on to become a member of the Royal College of Surgeons. Soon Gillies offered McIndoe a partnership at his Harley Street practice.

They performed hundreds of operations together in the 1930s and were pioneers of reconstructive cosmetic surgery. McIndoe helped perfect a breast reduction technique and pioneered a vaginoplasty surgical technique that was named after him.

Gillies recommended McIndoe as a first-class plastic surgeon and in 1938 Archie was appointed consultant in plastic surgery to the

Royal Air Force, succeeding Gillies. Archie accepted this position on the condition that he would be a civilian doctor, therefore not constricted by military rules and regulations; this stipulation was eventually accepted, but its advantage wasn't evident until later.

During the First World War, one million Commonwealth men had died and two million were injured. The Second World War was set to create similar brutal statistics. McIndoe was charged with trying to minimise the effects of war on the physical health of his patients, but in doing so he also pioneered ways of tending to their psychological health.

Sir Archibald Hector McIndoe (left) raising a toast to a former patient and his new bride in England

Archie set up a specialist hospital in East Sussex to treat 'airman's burn', caused when a plane's fuel tanks exploded, damaging an airman's exposed face and hands. Situated near France, McIndoe's unit received most of the air casualties and his team were dealing with patients as young as seventeen who had been trapped in fighter planes, where the cockpits amplified the heat and fire damage and could also act as a prison, burning or melting the young men's faces beyond recognition and oftentimes rendering them 'faceless'.

McIndoe did all he could to help these seemingly hopeless cases, treating several hundred men by skilfully performing difficult and painful reconstructive surgery on patients with deep burns and serious facial disfigurement. Although McIndoe was a quick and brilliant surgeon, facial reconstruction could take many surgeries (up to 70) over many months or years. As more and more of McIndoe's patients awaited their follow-up reconstructive surgery, they became known as 'McIndoe's Guinea Pig Club', in acknowledgement of the newness of this type of surgery.

But, from his work with Gillies in the 1930s, McIndoe knew that the world was unfairly biased against those considered ugly or deformed. He knew that although he could do a great deal to restore a semblance of normality to the visages of many of the men in his care, the world didn't take too kindly to those who appeared different. He also knew that this could deepen the already significant psychological damage that a veteran may go through when trying to establish a new life.

Archie recognised the part social reintegration could play in the rehabilitation of these men who would never look 'normal' again. He decided to ditch the hospital garb issued to his recuperating patients, and encouraged them to wear their civilian clothes or service uniforms while they were being treated at the hospital. In doing so, a more Kiwi-style camaraderie and mateship started to develop between patients and staff, and the confidence levels of the patients started to increase as did their trust in those charged with their care.

Indeed, McIndoe took this further, and often joined them for a beer (supplied by him) and a chat, asking their opinions on their future treatments. This dropping of the professional facade was just what the doctor ordered for many of the patients, who—already restricted by their injuries—were in need of regaining some self-esteem and independence.

While he performed the surgeries, McIndoe noticed a marked difference in the healing times of those soldiers who had ejected from their planes and into the sea and those who had ended up on dry land. It seems difficult to imagine now but the benefits of saline solution and its importance in medical procedures were not discovered until a Dunedin-born doctor observed that burnt airmen who had gone down in the ocean seemingly had less pain than similarly burnt airmen who had not had a sea-escape, and had burns that were clearer and easier and quicker to heal. From this observation, and after much testing, McIndoe pioneered the saline bath.

However, the problem of societal reintegration was still something that worried Archie McIndoe, and he knew how much the thought of putting their adjusted faces under public scrutiny daunted his patients, so he took it upon himself to find a way to ease the Guinea Pig Club members into the surrounding village life.

Doing what every sensible Kiwi bloke would do, he headed to the pub, and, chatting with the East Grinstead locals, he explained what he had been up to at the hospital ward, and told them about the disfigurement that his patients had suffered.

He advocated treating the patients as normal, urging the locals not to stare, and to approach them as they went for their strolls in the village. He even convinced some of the locals to accept his patients as guests and thus he pioneered a therapeutic community of people, foreshadowing social work practices of later decades. East Grinstead became 'the town that did not stare' and disfigured soldiers found it less traumatic returning to civilian life. McIndoe wasn't just the brains behind the integration, he put a lot of effort into organising social events with the community and patients, educating the village people with seminars, and putting on social and sporting activities for both villagers and patients to participate in.

First-class plastic surgeon and social welfare instigator, McIndoe employed people to help him with the reintegration projects; staff were hired not only for normal ward duties, but also to accompany servicemen to the pub or grocery store, or to advise them on financial and social matters and to assist in helping find new jobs or procuring job training for the officers whose limbs may have been maimed—somewhat like modern-day occupational therapy.

Archibald McIndoe, fondly referred to as 'the Maestro' by his staff and patients, was made CBE in 1944. After the war, he was conferred as a Commandeur de la Légion d'honneur (Commander of the Legion of Honour) and received his knighthood in 1947.

Having found fame and done good, he now pursued fortune and practised cosmetic surgery, working on famous faces such as Ava Gardner.

Not one to sit on his laurels, after visiting West Africa in 1947, Archie McIndoe decided to take up farming on the foothills of Mount Kilimanjaro, later establishing the African Medical and Research Foundation with two of his former students. This groundbreaking endeavour to provide medical assistance via flying doctors to remote areas of East Africa was inspired by Archie's resolve to counter the effects of poverty, tropical disease and isolation, and provide genuine and sustained healthcare for the communities. He realised that healthcare was not something that you could just throw money at, but by building up training and education, the damaging effects of large-scale ill-health could be countered.

Archibald McIndoe died in 1960, and his ashes were interred at the Royal Air Force church of St Clement Danes in Westminster, London.

Until 2007, the Guinea Pig Club met annually at East Grinstead, their anthem celebrates McIndoe's warmth and legacy:

*We are McIndoe's army,*
*We are his Guinea Pigs.*
*With dermatomes and pedicles,*
*Glass eyes, false teeth and wigs.*
*And when we get our discharge*
*We'll shout with all our might:*
*'Per ardua ad astra' **
*We'd rather drink than fight.*

*The RAF motto of 'through adversity to the stars'.

One of the founding Guinea Pig Club members Tom Cleave said:

> The biggest single achievement of the Guinea Pig Club is to have helped every member to save his face. His 'other' face, that is, in a psychological sense, so that he could securely take his place once more in society.

Archibald McIndoe may have been recognised by officialdom for his plastic surgery achievements, but it was this other saving of face that had the largest impact, not just on his patients, but on the community—including health workers.

One of his Guinea Pig Club graduates became a deputy medical officer of health, another patient who had been badly disfigured was so inspired by McIndoe that he returned to Queen Victoria Hospital as a fully qualified surgeon and trained under his former plastic surgeon, Archie McIndoe.

McIndoe got his own face time when he graced the cover of a 1948 edition of *Time* magazine.

# HAROLD GILLIES 1882–1960

*First to set the principles of modern plastic surgery*

We live in an appearance-obsessed society, yes, even in New Zealand, and if you say 'plastic surgery', people are likely to think of Hollywood-standardised ideals of age-defying beauty. However, despite millions of nose jobs and breast implants, the plastic surgery revolution had its genesis in the wounded faces of First World War veterans.

The history of plastic surgery can be traced back more than 4000 years, with practitioners in India and Egypt first recording skin grafts, and Romans reconstructing ears that had been swiped off during gladiatorial-type battle in the first century BC.

The adjective plastic derives from the Greek πλαστική, *plastikē*, and denotes the sculpting of malleable material. The traditional skin-graft technique was to stitch the edges of wounds together, which meant that when scar tissue contracted facial features were disfigured and twisted.

The shrapnel produced by high explosives and heavy artillery used in the First World War, along with trench warfare that left soldiers' heads more exposed than the rest of the body, meant an unprecedented number of horrific facial injuries, with thousands of young men's faces often shattered or burnt beyond recognition. These men, who had left home fresh faced and full of optimism, suffered disfiguring wounds and—often unable to see, hear, speak, eat or drink—found it difficult to return to normal civilian life.

Operating out of Aldershot hospital in England, New Zealander Harold Delf Gillies began performing operations which involved rebuilding the face by taking tissue from other parts of the body. He was to become the man considered by many to be the father of plastic surgery.

Harold Gillies was the youngest of eight children and was born in Dunedin in 1882. His father had died when Harold was four, but had left enough money to enable Harold to attend prep school in England before attending Wanganui Collegiate and then Cambridge to study medicine.

As a boy, Harold was diligent and dextrous, and he captained the Wanganui Collegiate first eleven in 1900 and was named the best young player in the country that year. He was also an accomplished artist, and this artistry enhanced and informed his later profession.

When the First World War broke out, Gillies joined the Red Cross and was sent to Belgium. He met with a French physician who was experimenting with taking tissue from other parts of the body to treat jaw wounds. This process captured Harold Gillies' imagination and he realised that he wanted to work in reconstructive rather than general surgery. Seeing the results of war first-hand at the Front, Harold asked for the British Army to set up a plastic-surgery unit and to be posted there. Gillies was the first surgeon in charge of Britain's first plastic-surgery unit.

Although grafting skin from an undamaged part of the body to the face was a known procedure, the risk of infection was very high and this also increased the likelihood of large-scale scarring and disfigurement. Blood types were just becoming known, blood transfusions were also in the early stages, and antibiotics had not yet been invented (they were developed in the late 1920s).

Harold wasn't afraid of trying new techniques, and it was mid-way through treating able seaman Willie Vicarage, whose ship had been hit eight times and whose jaw was completely demolished, that Gillies pioneered the 'tubed pedicle' technique. Cutting a flap of skin from the chest or forehead, Gillies noted that the cut skin would naturally curl inwards. He then 'swung' the still-attached skin flap into place over the face but stitched the flap into a tube which allowed the blood supply to flow between graft and injured skin as well as dramatically reducing the chances of infection. Tubular 'pedicles' could be fashioned from the forehead, scalp, chest, neck or shoulders but retained a connection to allow blood flow; this was a revolution and soon became a commonplace procedure.

Gillies believed that plastic surgery should not only restore function, but also form—he wanted to eliminate deformity as much as possible. Before Gillies came to the forefront of plastic surgery, although they did their best, surgeons had very little concern for final aesthetics and many soldiers left the operating table mended, but hideously disfigured.

Gillies' sense of aesthetics meant that he was very concerned with restoring his patients' looks, which he realised would help them reintegrate into civilian life. Before each operation, Harold would spend an hour visualising the final outcome, sketching on pieces of paper, cutting them out, and then fitting them back together. He'd work a lump of wax as a veritable rough draft of what he hoped to achieve on the operating table, carefully moulding the contours and form of a patient's new face.

Gillies kept trying new techniques, once crafting a soldier's new nose from the soldier's rib cartilage and a skin flap from his forehead. The process took at least six months, but years later, the skin of the new nose was said to flush just like a normal one would when the man blushed.

Although very successful, Gillies sometimes had patients that were too damaged and his operations were too ambitious; when an attempt to mend a very advanced facial damage victim using a large flap of skin failed and the patient didn't survive, Gillies realised he had tried to take on too much too quickly. But he didn't give up; he recognised this as a lesson to be learned and from this developed the staged grafts technique, the gradual rebuilding process that is the basis of all plastic surgery performed today. Writing in his journal, Gillies noted, 'never do today, what can be honourably put off till tomorrow'.

In 1917, Gillies opened a purpose-built hospital with 1000 beds for the treatment of the facially wounded at Queen Mary's Hospital in Kent where Harold and his colleagues carried out more than 11,000 operations on over 5000 men.

Between the wars, Harold set up a private practice on London's Harley Street and went on a worldwide teaching and demonstration circuit. He engaged in and encouraged innovation, and one of his enduring legacies is the multi-disciplinary team; when operating on a face, Gillies found that a dental surgeon's expertise was helpful and that establishing a collaborative relationship between the general surgeon and the plastic surgeon was of vital importance to the success of many cases. In the 1930s, his relative and fellow Kiwi, Archibald McIndoe (see page 139), trained under him. Harold Gillies was knighted in 1930.

Between the wars, Gillie's reputation as an aesthete led many who didn't 'need' surgery, but 'wanted' it, to his door. People of society, actors and film stars sought Harold's skilled hands in 'lifting' their faces to be more youthful or camera friendly.

One of Harold's patients was a young child who, at four years old, had suffered severe facial scarring in a roadside accident and whose face had been coated with boiling tar and bitumen. Jean Dawnay's operation was a huge success and was reported in *The Lancet*. In the 1950s, Jean later went on to be a successful model for Dior, and kept company with the likes of Grace Kelly in Majorca; like Ms Kelly, Jean even ended up marrying a prince (she is now known as Princess Jean Galitzine and her daughter is 612th in line to the British throne).

Sadly, peacetime frivolity was broken by another war. Plastic surgery was again 'needed'. At the outbreak of the Second World War, there were only three experienced plastic surgeons in Britain: Gillies, McIndoe and Rainsford Mowlem, all three of them New Zealanders, all three of them headed multi-disciplinary surgical teams.

Gillies carried out the first female-to-male sex reassignment surgery in 1946. This first transsexual patient was Laurence Michael Dillon (known as Michael and born Laura Maud Dillon). Five years later, Gillies performed the first sex reassignment surgery from male-to-female, pioneering a flap technique on Roberta Cowell which became the standard for 40 years. Before the operation, when Roberta had been known as Robert, she had been a Spitfire pilot in the Second World War and a racing driver after the war. Michael later became a physician and penned a book that investigated transsexuality. He and Roberta became friends after being introduced by Harold Gillies.

Harold Gillies accomplished so many firsts, and continued to share his teachings until just before his death in London in 1960.

The American Academy of Facial Plastic and Reconstructive Surgery recognises this Kiwi pioneer's huge contribution with its annual Harold Delf Gillies Award for Best Science Research Paper.

# MIKE McMANAWAY 1961–

*First to tangle us with Tantrix*

Mike McManaway is an outdoor sort—he studied geography at the University of Canterbury and his interests include climbing, paragliding and caving. This does not explain why he is the inventor of New Zealand's most successful tabletop game, Tantrix. Perhaps it goes some way, though, because it was while McManaway was sitting in a tent, nursing a broken collarbone after a climbing accident in South America, that he came up with the idea and prototype that was to evolve into the game.

The hugely popular game, which has now sold more than 50 million plastic tiles in the two decades since it was invented, was originally called Mind Game, after the games shop that McManaway owned. It is a hexagonal tile-based abstract game and its 56 different tiles have three lines painted on them, going from one edge of the tile to another. No two lines on a tile have the same colour. There are four colours in the set: red, yellow, blue and green.

Going on a hunch that his idea may make for a successful game, and while recovering from the climbing fall, in 1988, Mike got a South American manufacturer to produce cardboard tiles for a two-player game. Back in his garage in Heathcote, Christchurch, with collarbone tended to, McManaway hand-painted the first 100,000 cardboard pieces with only two coloured lines, red and black—good Canterbury colours.

McManaway sold the game through his store and following customer feedback continued to change the rules and design. In 1991, the tiles were changed to plastic and two more colours were added, allowing for four-player games. He says, 'It was not a company in the beginning, it was my hobby.'

According to Mike, Tantrix's success is due to it being a family and strategy game, which requires some luck to win. 'Luck is where the addiction comes in. An eight-year-old could do rather well. They will usually lose to you, but they can win and that's what keeps them interested.' However, there are clever ways to influence the luck factor. Even though he invented the game, it still took Mike ten years of persistent attempts to win the World Tantrix Championship in 2007. Tantrix is now sold in more than 30 countries, has multiple versions, and a very competitive online community.

## ZORBING

Rolling down hills is a favourite childhood activity, but why does it have to be little kids who have all the fun? Two Kiwi blokes, Andrew Akers and software engineer Dwane van der Sluis, were looking for some new adventure so came up with the idea of Zorbing, a unique activity involving rolling down a hill in a giant inflatable plastic ball. These enormous orbs, sometimes known as spheres or Zorbs, are double-skinned inflatable balls into which a willing passenger can enter the inner core and roll down hilly terrain while protected by the air-cushioned outer core. As the sphere rolls, at speeds of up to 50 kilometres per hour, the passenger's head goes over heels, but the build-up of centrifugal force keeps them pressed hard against the transparent plastic wall, allowing for an exhilarating sightseeing adventure.

Andrew put his hands up to be the first tester of the Zorb, and the first downhill ball rolling occurred at Akers' family farm near Kawarau, followed by a more public outing on One Tree Hill's volcanic cone.

Since its invention, the Zorb has been featured on UK TV show *Top Gear*, musician Peter Gabriel has performed inside one on his 2003 tour of Europe and America, and zorbing has been featured on *The Amazing Race*, *The Late Show with David Letterman* and the Discovery Channel. In 2006, the company split and Andrew started Ogo, which developed further zorb products. During the development of zorbing there have been a few moments of clarity and hilarity: as a marketing ploy, males who chose to go zorbing naked were able to roll for free. However, it seemed too many men were keen to go with the flow, and nude zorbing was ceased. Receiving a request from Jet Propulsion Laboratories (see page 22) to use the balls for NASA research into Mars landings, Andrew initially thought it a joke and dismissed the request. NASA is still investigating using a zorb-like inflatable vehicle called the Tumbleweed Rover to propel a robotic reconnoiter vehicle across the Martian plains using wind power. Back on planet Earth, the sensation of weightlessness that zorb participants enjoy led to the term 'zorbonauts'.

Zorbing entered the *Concise Oxford English Dictionary* (see Robert Burchfield—page 244) in 2001 where it was defined as 'a sport in which a participant is secured inside an inner capsule in a large, transparent ball which is then rolled along the ground or down hills'.

The flagship site in Rotorua is now the permanent home of Zorbing and sees over 50,000 people a year roll down a hill, 730,000 since 1995, and the Ogo company has been franchised to various fun-park sites around the world.

# 7

# FIRST TO THE TABLE

## FOOD AND WINE AND BEER!

Kiwis love their lawns and the first meadow grass was sown in Kerikeri on 20 July 1821 by the Reverend John Butler. It was no easy take; to do this he had to clear a section of fern that he claimed was seven foot high. He also planted other crops:

> I have seven acres of wheat, and six of barley and oats, growing at this time, all looking remarkably well . . . Also my garden is full of a variety of vegetables and young fruit trees, and an excellent bed of hops . . . also one potato house, thirty feet by ten. One new fowl-house, twenty-one by ten. One goat house, eight by ten.

Apples and pear trees brought from New South Wales were first planted by Reverend Samuel Marsden in 1819 on the Church Missionary Society station in Kerikeri. He also planted grapes, plums and peaches that year. One of the pear trees that still exists in Kerikeri is officially New Zealand's first introduced tree.

Kumara was the nation's first staple food, introduced by Maori. Later, in 1774, Captain Cook decided to plant some seeds to create an extended vege patch which he hoped would be useful for further excursions.

Marsden Cross Historic Memorial Reserve at Rangihoua Bay on the Purerua Peninsula commemorates where Rev Marsden held New Zealand's first Christian sermon in 1814. But there is also a memorial to Thomas Hansen, New Zealand's first non-missionary European settler, who planted a lemon tree that has recently been rediscovered—DoC has plans to propagate it in time for the descendants of Thomas to celebrate at the Hansen family bicentenary in 2014. The first lemon trees were planted to help combat scurvy in ships' crews.

## THE BEST THING SINCE SLICED BREAD

*The first cheese rolls*

It's a Southern thing. North Islanders are missing out on a food group that only South Islanders seem to know about. The Otago/Southern cheese roll is a toasted snack of sliced white bread rolled up with a cheesy, savoury, precooked filling. The earliest recipe for what has become known as the Otago cheese roll was published in the *New Zealand Truth* in 1935. The earliest known cookbook entry for this favourite delicacy dates from Dunedin's Roslyn Church Jubilee Cookery Book in 1951, and cheese rolls have been on the menu at the Little Hut Cafe on Dunedin's George Street since 1955, around about the time when sliced bread became commercially available, and subsequently the popularity of cheese rolls rocketed. The electric toasted sandwich maker first made its appearance in New Zealand between 1973 and 1974.

# WINE

*First vintage*

Samuel Marsden planted the first grapevines for wine at the missionary station in Kerikeri in 1819. On his second visit to New Zealand, Marsden recorded the planting in his journal:

> We had a small spot of land cleared and broken up, in which I planted about a hundred grape vines of different kinds brought from Port Jackson. New Zealand promises to be very favourable to the vine, as far as I can judge at the present of the nature of the soil and climate. Should the vine succeed it will prove of vast importance in this part of the globe.

The first à la carte restaurant was the Hi-Diddle-Griddle which opened in 1952 on the then classy Karangahape Road in Auckland. Patrons could enjoy dinner, some music and later dancing. Though not a bottle of wine.

The now ubiquitous wine list was not even an option on the New Zealand restaurant scene until 1961. In 1954, Dutch-born Otto Groen, opened up Gourmet on Shortland Street. Having recently arrived in New Zealand he was a bit shocked that wine and beer were only served with food in hotels while the bars were open.

So Otto instituted the practice of immediately serving iced water to diners. Well-prepared and thirsty patrons could then use the water glasses to enjoy the wine they had smuggled in under their jackets. Groen's restaurant was repeatedly raided by police, and he was convicted four times for breaking liquor licensing laws.

For seven years, Groen battled to provide the sort of hospitality that he knew his customers wanted, and finally, after meeting with Prime Minister Sir Walter Nash in 1961, Gourmet became New Zealand's first licensed restaurant. The very Kiwi institution of BYO was not legal until 1976.

In 1979, Vidal's in Hawke's Bay extended wine and food matching by opening New Zealand's first restaurant at a vineyard.

In 1963, New Zealand's first major export of wine was from Auckland winemakers, Corbans.

# BEER

*First brew*

On 23 March 1773, Captain James Cook started to brew the first beer in this country at Dusky Sound (see page 206). Using branches of a spruce tree in his decoction, Captain Cook intended the beer to be a tonic against scurvy for his crew. The fresh shoots of many spruces and pines are a natural source of vitamin C. The sugar-based beer was ready four days later.

Sixty-two years after Cook's first-draft draught, New Zealand's first commercial brewery was established in 1835 by Joel Samuel Polack—one of the first Jewish settlers, and a well-regarded recorder of precolonial New Zealand—in Kororareka (now Russell). For a taste of what Captain Cook's crew were imbibing, head to Golden Bay's Mussel Inn where they make a variation of the amber brew under the name Captain Cooker.

CAPTAIN COOK'S METHOD OF MAKING SPRUCE BEER.
*We at first made our beer of a decoction of the spruce leaves; but, finding that this alone made it too astringent, we afterwards mixed with it an equal quantity of the tea plant (a name it obtained in my former voyage, from our using it as a tea then, as we also did now), which partly destroyed the astringency of the other, and made the beer exceedingly palatable, and esteemed by every one on board. We brewed it in the same manner as spruce beer, and the process is as follows. First make a strong decoction of the small branches of the spruce and tea-plants, by boiling them three*

*or four hours, or until the bark will strip with ease from the branches; then take them out of the copper, and put in the proper quantity of molasses, ten gallons of which is sufficient to make a ton, or two hundred and forty gallons of beer. Let this mixture just boil; then put it into casks, and to it add an equal quantity of cold water, more or less according to the strength of the decoction, or your taste. When the whole is milk-warm, put in a little grounds of beer, or yeast if you have it, or anything else that will cause fermentation, and in a few days the beer will be fit to drink.*

*Any one who is in the least acquainted with spruce pines will find the tree which I have distinguished by that name. There are three sorts of it: that which has the smallest leaves and deepest colour is the sort we brewed with, but doubtless all three might safely serve that purpose.*

—*Cook's Second Voyage towards the South Pole, 4th edition, vol. 1*

The three spruces here referred to were probably the rimu, the kahikatea, and the mai or matai, which are different species of *Dacryds*.

# CHAU TSEUNG (CHEW CHONG) 1827–44?–1920

*First mushroom exporter*

*The first to create the iconic pound of butter*

One of the first privately owned dairy factories in New Zealand was opened by a Chinese-born man who had previously been responsible for Taranaki's reputation as the 'fungus province'. Chew Chong arrived in

Otago in 1867, and unlike many Chinese men of the time he wasn't involved in the hunt for precious metal, but instead collected scrap metal and exported it back to China.

In 1870, when he was 42 years old, Chew Chong headed north to Taranaki, where he noticed in the forests of tawa and mahoe an edible fungus, *Auricularia polytricha*, growing. In Chinese the mushroom is called mu er (Wood Ear), in Maori it is called hakeka. Chong realised this fungus (also known as woodear, Jew's ear, edible jelly fungus, edible fungus and Taranaki wool) was valued in Chinese medicine and would have a ready market. He travelled the countryside by horse and cart as a peddler, selling various goods and buying fungus. Chong started to export the Taranaki wool in large quantities to Chinese populations in Australia, China and California. He encouraged impoverished Taranaki farming families to harvest the fungus and this source of cash meant that the fungus was soon termed Egmont Gold and Black Gold, and—easily able to be collected by women and children—became a principal income source for many local families. Between 1874 and 1881, the annual

Chew Chong, innovative entrepreneur, was honoured by dairymen from all over Taranaki during a ceremony in 1910

export value of fungus exceeded that of butter—but this was before refrigerated shipments which created a big dairy export boom. Chew's export business helped finance Chong's next endeavour—opening a general store in 1873 on the corner of Devon and Currie streets in New Plymouth.

He became a successful and well-regarded businessman, also opening a couple of butcheries, three more general stores and, in 1887, a dairy factory—the Riverside Butter Factory, later renamed Jubilee Factory— near Eltham.

In those days butter was made from a blend from different farms; the quality of this 'milled butter' was unreliable, because a whole batch could be contaminated if one faulty butter was blended in.

Butter was not sold in any conventional size, but was sold in pats and blobs. Chew realised that butter needed to be more consistent in size and in hygiene if it was to be exported, so he started marketing butter in one-pound blocks and wrapped them in parchment paper. He also installed a cooling system to gain further control over quality and hygiene.

At the New Zealand and South Seas International Exhibition in 1889–90, Chong's efforts were recognised when he won the Class A butter competition for producing the best butter suitable for export.

Chew Chong was an entrepreneurial influence in the Eltham area in particular and the Taranaki district in general—during the 1891–92 influenza epidemic he offered Taranaki residents free acupuncture treatment, and he was generous in civic spirit, donating a flag pole to the New Plymouth recreation grounds.

Chew married a local Taranaki girl, Elizabeth Whatton, and together they raised a large family. Chew was formally recognised by prominent citizens for his export trade in fungus and butters in 1910. He died in 1920 at the age of 92.

His early business nous was posthumously recognised when in 1988 he was inducted into the New Zealand Business Hall of Fame. The silver cup that he won at the New Zealand exhibition, along with a few other artefacts, are on display in Taranaki's beautiful museum Puke Ariki. And a recreation of his butcher's shop is on display at the unusual, engaging and imaginative Tawhiti Museum near Hawera.

## SPREADABLE BUTTER

In 1991, after nearly two decades of research, the New Zealand Dairy Research Institute introduced spreadable butter to the world. They developed a method of 'fractionation' whereby liquid butter-fat is recombined with solid butter to make a spreadable consistency—but it had taken years to find a way to make the process commercially viable on a large scale. Spreadable butter made its world debut in the UK, and after proving successful there, it was soon seen in New Zealand fridges—making the once ubiquitous butter conditioner a thing of the past as well as saving millions of people needless frustration when struggling to spread fridge-cold lumps of butter on morning toast.

A special $1 New Zealand Post stamp was issued in 2007 celebrating spreadable butter as one of the greatest Kiwi inventions of all time.

# MURIEL BELL 1898–1974

*First state nutritionist responsible for increasing our awareness
of how what we eat and drink affects our wellbeing*

Muriel Bell was not only the first woman to be awarded a medical doctorate by the University of Otago in 1926, for her research work on the relationship between the enlarged thyroid gland and the basal metabolic rate which lead to the nationwide iodisation of salt, but she was also the first state nutritionist.

A head girl at Nelson College for Girls, Muriel started her academic career with a BA at Victoria University. She then transferred to the medical school at Otago—where she later became a lecturer of physiology and one of the first female academics at Otago medical school.

Muriel was appointed as the first nutrition officer in the Department of Health in 1940, as well as simultaneously being the director of nutrition research at the Otago medical school. In her role as state nutritionist she helped to educate the public health sector, Plunket nurses and the public at large about the importance of improving nutrition to better our general health and wellbeing.

As nutrition advisor and advocate she increased awareness of the need for milk in children's and adults' diets—promoting free school milk as 'our best single food'—as a key factor in creating healthy bones and teeth. Further to promoting strong teeth, Muriel was one of the leading proponents for the fluoridation of water, and she also spearheaded research into the diets of basic wage earners and conducted surveys on Maori diets in the early 1940s.

Muriel was responsible for setting the national ration scales for food items during the Second World War and prepared the rations not only for the men involved in Edmund Hillary's Trans-Antarctic expedition in 1956–57 (see page 52), but also the dogs.

A saviour of bottlefed babies, Muriel revised the Plunket feeding tables ensuring a more protein-rich formula and lower fat content, as well as developing formula for babies with milk allergies.

Although twice married (and widowed), and stepmother to seven, Muriel Bell kept her maiden name, having built up her research reputation before her marriages.

Muriel made a vital contribution to New Zealand public health, with founding research on New Zealand soil deficiencies, and research into cholesterol and heart disease, and she presented the information in easily accessible ways, including in magazine articles and radio broadcasts. She also did research on bush sickness in sheep for the newly established DSIR.

A woman with foresight, Muriel urged insurance companies to collect statistics on obesity and advocated a primary healthcare focus on Maori and Pasifika dietary patterns.

She became a fellow of the Royal Society of New Zealand in 1952, the Royal Society of Medicine, and the Royal Australasian College of Physicians and appointed a CBE in 1959. In 1968 she was awarded an honorary doctorate from the University of Otago, and praised for her 'unexampled energy to make the findings of research available for the common benefit'. She died in May 1974 in Dunedin.

# 8

# BIRTHS, DEATHS AND UNIONS

## THOMAS HOLLOWAY KING 1815–18

*The first European (Pakeha) child born in New Zealand*

There must have been many 'firsts' witnessed by both Maori and European cultures when the two started to mix and mingle in the nineteenth century. Hannah King—the only woman from the first 1814 settlement of the Church Missionary Society to remain in New Zealand for the rest of her life—would have seen quite a few in her first years in her new home. She, her husband John and their one-year-old son arrived on board the brig *Active*, along with Samuel Marsden, three other missionary families, three convict labourers, Marsden's mate John Liddiard Nicholas and several Maori returning to Aotearoa. Also on board the vessel anchored in Rangihoua Bay on 22 December 1814 were the first chooks to be introduced to New Zealand.

Hannah was so heavily pregnant at the time that she was lowered in a wooden chair from the *Active* to a waiting rowboat. Just a few months later, at age 22, Hannah gave birth to Thomas Holloway King, the first European to be born in New Zealand. A few days before the birth, John King stated it would be a blessing if the primitive conditions of the hut, a raupo whare (reed hut) where they were temporarily living, did not affect his wife and noted that she had a cold; the lack of chimney or windows, and flimsy nature of the cladding was next to useless for keeping the tropical rains from falling on their heads.

A few months later, this passage by John Nicholas, recording the birth of Thomas King in New Zealand on 21 February 1815, is an insight into the two cultures eyeing each other up, unsure of what the future may hold, but giving it (and sometimes each other) a bash anyway.

The wife of Mr. King was delivered on this day of a fine boy; and I was first informed of the circumstance by one of the natives, a man who acted as servant to her mother, Mrs Hanson. This fellow, who would have made an excellent buffoon, as he possessed all the requisite humour for such a character, met me . . . and telling me that Mrs. King had got a pickeeninee, (a child) he began to describe her groans and expressions while suffering under the pains of labour; and there was such an air of droll mockery in the indecent representation, that I could not forbear laughing heartily, though I desired him to desist from so unseemly a detail. He descanted in a strain of arch ridicule on the extreme timidity of our countrywomen in this situation, compared with the hardy resolution of the New Zealand ladies. The latter, he said, never experienced any inconvenience from childbirth; but sitting down in the open air, surrounded by a concourse of both sexes, were delivered without uttering a single groan, while the spectators, who stood carefully watching the process, shouted out tarnee! tarnee! (an infant, an infant) as soon as nature had executed her office; when the mother, after cutting the umbilical cord, rose up as if no such occurrence had taken place, and resumed her ordinary occupations. But, said he, 'Europee woman be no like New Zealand woman; she cry out, Measser King! Measser King! for ittee ittee tarnee' meaning that his countrywomen would have more spirit than to use such an exclamation in so trifling affair as the delivery of a little infant.

—John Nicholas, *Narrative of a Voyage to New Zealand in the Years 1814 and 1815*

It's a shame that the event has no record penned by Hannah or other female in attendance. For her second-born's baptism, Hannah clothed Thomas in a fine embroidered gown, which is now held in the historic collection at Te Waimate Mission House, Waimate North.

Rev Marsden recorded the event of the baptism which also incorporated New Zealand's first recorded commercial land transaction:

Three days previous to this Mrs King was delivered of a fine boy, who was brought out and publicly baptized at the same time the deed was executed upon this newly purchased land. All these circumstances at such a juncture were very interesting to us and will be long remembered by the natives. The price paid for the land was twelve axes.

—*The Letters and Journals of Samuel Marsden, 1765–1838*

Nicholas elaborated:

> As this was the last day of our being on shore, we were careful in leaving nothing undone that was connected with our visit to the island, and necessary to be settled before our departure. The land, therefore, on which the missionaries had erected their dwellings was now regularly purchased . . .
>
> Before we repaired on board, Mr Marsden baptised, in the presence of the natives, the child of which Mrs King had been lately delivered; and they evinced during the ceremony, a kind of fearful apprehension for the safety of the infant, mingled with astonishment at the rites they beheld, but behaved at the same time with the greatest propriety . . .

Twelve axes for 200 acres—would it be too contentious to say, 'what a steal'?

Unfortunately, little Thomas only lived until the age of three and a half years; on 12 November 1818, missionary William Hall recorded that 'Mr King's little boy has for some time past laboured under a lung wasting disease and this morning he fell asleep and awoke no more in this world for ever.'

Hannah King remained in New Zealand, teaching Maori girls and raising nine healthy children. Her grave can be found at the Christ Church Cemetery, Russell, Bay of Islands.

# FIRST CHRISTMAS/CHRISTIAN CEREMONY ON NEW ZEALAND SOIL

On Christmas Day of 1815, Samuel Marsden held the first recorded Christian service on New Zealand soil at Oihi Bay. The local chief, Ruatara, who had met Marsden on a ship returning to Australia from England, interpreted the sermon for his people. (This occasion inspired the Willow Macky composition *Te Harinui*, New Zealand's best-loved Christmas carol, and first performed in New Zealand by an Australian choir in 1959—wouldn't you know it? The first recording of the song was presented to Samuel Marsden's direct descendant and namesake in 1964. No end-of-the-year primary school assembly is without this much-loved song being sung at full gusto.)

Although Marsden's service is known for commemorating the first official New Zealand Christmas, it is probable that French explorer Jean François Marie de Surville and his crew, which included a Dominican priest, had a sacred and merry celebration of their own aboard the vessel *Saint Jean Baptiste*, anchored in Doubtless Bay on 25 December 1769. Although there are no records of this, it is unlikely that such an important Catholic occasion would have gone by without ceremony.

Semantics comes in to play here; Marsden's was the first *recorded* service on *soil*.

## FIRST CHRISTMAS MEALS

In late December 1642, Abel Tasman and the crew on the Dutch ships *Heemskerck* and *Zeehaen* anchored east of Stephens and D'Urville islands, and a Christmas pork dinner along with a fair bit of yuletide wine helped them bide their time waiting out a Wellington weather bomb before their planned crossing of Cook Strait.

In stormy seas at the tip of the country in 1769, James Cook and his *Endeavour* crew feasted on 'Goose pye'. Perhaps the Kiwi version of 'Twelve Days of Christmas' should be adapted so that it honours the gannet that Joseph Banks, the ship's botanist, shot for the meal, and which stood in for the 'goose'.

## FIRST INTER-RACIAL MARRIAGE (AND FIRST CHRISTIAN WEDDING CEREMONY AND FIRST RECORDED MAORI BAPTISM)

The first (Christian) wedding ceremony took place on 23 June 1823—the marriage also ended that day when the bride bolted for the bush.

Hans Homan Jensen Falk was a Dutch mariner, trader and whaler who became known as Phillip Tapsell (topsail). Whaling brought him repeatedly to the Bay of Islands, and on one visit in 1823, while serving on the *Asp*, he asked missionary Thomas Kendall to officiate a marriage ceremony between him and Maria Ringa of Nga Puhi. Maria had to be baptised before Kendall could sanctify the marriage, and this is the first recorded Maori baptism to Christianity.

Although this event was sanctioned by the church, it was not a marriage made in heaven—the bride obviously wasn't that into her groom or the ceremony and left Phillip later that day.

Thomas Kendall received a bit of flack and was dismissed from the mission by Samuel Marsden who condemned him for performing the ceremony which could then be seen as a church-sanctioned inter-racial marriage. Marsden also believed that Maria's reasons for being baptised—and thus converting to Christianity—were muddled with the marriage.

Philip Tapsell bought the steaming White Island for two barrels of rum

Phillip had two more tries at marriage after apparently learning that his first wife was now dead; in April 1830, Phillip's second marriage ceremony was this time performed by Samuel Marsden himself, who had obviously reconciled with the idea of inter-racial marriage. Philip married Karuhi, sister of Nga Puhi chief Wharepoaka. The couple settled down and Philip started life as a trader in military arms.

Karuhi died soon after and Philip's third marriage was to a high-ranking woman of Ngati Whakaue of Te Arawa. The marriage with Hine-i-turama Ngatiki was originally a Maori ceremony but was later sanctified, this time by Bishop Pompallier, and the couple ended up having six children.

Phillip was also the first non-Maori 'owner' of White Island—having bought the sulphurous volcano for two hogsheads (barrels) of rum in 1839.

Phillip was a bit of a rover whose tales of adventure and misadventure were serialised in the *Daily Southern Cross* in 1869. *Events in the Life of Phillip Tapsell, Old Dane* makes for an entertaining and fascinating (although somewhat unreliable) insight into the experiences of a whaler and firearms trader making a new life in this new land.

A determined fellow, at the age of 90, he walked the 65 kilometres between Maketu and Whakatane when he heard that the Duke of Edinburgh was coming to New Zealand. He was 96 when he died. Descendants of Phillip include former Cabinet minister Sir Peter Tapsell.

One hundred and eighty two years later, after the Civil Union Act was passed John Jolliff and Des Smith were one of the first New Zealand couples to celebrate their civil union in Wellington on 1 May 2005. Before the union, Jolliff joked with the media that, 'There may be nothing borrowed, nothing blue, but there will be a couple of old buggers and something new.' (See Bugger, page 74.)

Six and a half years after that day, and 2486 civil unions later, Piri Norris and Justin Elder made New Zealand history when they had the first civil ceremony in the Legislative Council Chamber of Parliament—the very place people had fought for same-sex relationships to be legally recognised.

# FIRST DIVORCE

In 1867, the first New Zealand law allowing people to apply for divorce was passed. The only grounds for divorce was adultery by either spouse, but only if there were additional aggravating circumstances (for example, a spouse may have to prove that their partner had inflicted violence or abuse). Prior to 1867, conflicted couples had to apply to British courts. In 1868 there was one application for divorce. In 1900 there were 111, although rates of desertion were not recorded. Desertion became an additional ground for divorce in 1898.

In what appears to be the first case of divorce, Mr William and Mrs Marian Oldrey's case for child custody appeared before the Supreme Court on 20 August 1869. The application did not proceed as Mrs Oldrey was in the process of arranging a judicial separation.

APPLICATION FOR DIVORCE.
*It would appear that the sittings of the Supreme Court under the Divorce and Matrimonial Causes Act, at Wellington, next month, will have some business brought before it. Proceedings under the Act have already been initiated by a gentleman well known in this city for a dissolution of marriage,*

*on the ground of adultery by his wife. And another distinct petition has been made by the wife for a judicial separation from her husband, on the ground of cruelty. The husband's petition sets forth that his wife has committed adultery at various times with a certain respectable young gentleman, and that she is at present living in adultery with him. The wife's petition sets forth that I the husband has been guilty of violent acts of cruelty towards her, extending over a period of three years, and states that, although before compelled to leave him for a time in consequence of his cruelty, she was induced to condone the various acts and to return to him, upon his promising to behave better in the future. She had again been compelled to fly from her husband with her children last Saturday week, and to seek refuge with her father and mother, with whom she has remained up to the present time, she prays for a judicial separation, and the custody of the children.*

—*Daily Southern Cross*, 18 August 1869

## ENABLING FIRST BREATH FOR PREMATURE BABIES

One of New Zealand's most significant contributions to the medical world came about after a chat over the back paddock fence. A farmer neighbour of Graham 'Mont' Liggins asked the obstetrician what he thought caused the high incidence of lamb deaths after premature delivery triggered by dogs worrying ewes. Mont did not know, but he suspected it had something to do with cortisol—the natural stress-response steroid.

He realised that solving this question may have a big impact on the mortality rate of premature human births.

In a series of experiments he proved his hypothesis that foetal cortisol release triggered labour and he also noted that often the lungs of premature lambs did not inflate due to a lack of a surfactant, therefore increasing the chance of developing respiratory distress syndrome (RDS). Yet, Mont—whose nickname came about after a childhood obsession with Monty Mouse (the Disney predecessor of Mickey Mouse)—observed sheep on Auckland's One Tree Hill and saw that if a ewe was given corticosteroids prior to delivery, normal lung functionality was achieved.

Recognising that one of the biggest killers of newborn babies is respiratory distress, the result of immature lungs, Mont Liggins and his small team focused on this.

Over the next few years this hypothesis was tested in human premature labours—the occurrence of RDC and death was dramatically reduced and the simple treatment is now used to save the lives and prevent brain damage of thousands of premature babies annually. Mont's work in the 1960s and 1970s established Auckland's National Women's Hospital as a world-leading centre for the care of mothers and babies.

Yet, this revolutionarily simple treatment was not adopted straight away—the esteemed medical journal *The Lancet* even rejecting publication of Mont's paper on the grounds that it would be of little general interest. It took a further two decades before Mont's exceptionally methodical and well-documented research was implemented throughout the western medical world and his work was acknowledged worldwide as one of the greatest single contributions to the advancement of human health.

The son of a doctor, Graham 'Mont' Collingwood Liggins was born 24 June 1926 in Thames, studied medicine in Dunedin, and furthered his studies in the UK, where he met his wife Celia—who was Auckland's first female obstetrician.

He became professor of obstetrics and gynaecological endocrinology at the University of Auckland in 1968. In 2001, when the university established the first major institute dedicated to developmental research, it was named after him. The Liggins Institute is a world-leading centre for research on foetal and child health, nutritional health, growth and development, and breast cancer medicine.

His career was that of a successful number-eight-wire innovative Kiwi—pioneering, proactive and with the ability to understand that the answer may be in the unanticipated or as yet unasked question.

He was appointed CBE in 1983, knighted in 1991 and died in August 2010. Full of vim and vigour and grand schemes, Mont installed a solar panel watering system for his veggie patch before he died of lymphoma. Celia blamed the lymphatic cancer on the regular swims that Mont had taken by the nuclear power plant at Windscale, Newcastle upon Tyne, when they had first met in the UK.

# 9

# MOUNTAINS/LAKES/OCEANS/RIVERS

## WAVES

Being surrounded by the sea in a temperate zone and having strong prevailing westerly winds in winter, New Zealand is one of the countries with the most potential to channel wave energy. This realistically usable worldwide resource, which has the potential to economically power our homes with minimal environmental damage, is not a new idea and the first patent for a device that could harness the power of the waves goes back to Paris in 1799.

But in 1903 a Dunedin inventor patented New Zealand's first device capable of 'obtaining a workable power of commercial value from the force exerted by the action or movement of the waves'.

Robert Miller stretched a suspended wire cable across a cove south of St Clair beach, to which he attached a floating pontoon of logs, which was then attached by a pulley mechanism to a machine on the beach. As the waves rose or fell, the resulting push and pull of friction produced about 1 horsepower of energy. With every movement of the pontoon creating energy, Miller estimated that a 500-tonne pontoon could supply more than 500 horsepower and a whole series of pontoons would provide unlimited power.

Although Mr Miller's invention was not a commercial success, it is worth noting that it appeared at the beginning of the age of petrol. Now, at the end of the petroleum age, perhaps another Kiwi will come up with a less-cumbersome and more readily adaptable way to harness this natural and renewable resource. Other countries have wave farms and the potential for electricity generation from clean water reservoirs filled with natural-wave powered desalination plants is on the horizon.

## LEGENDARY SWIM

The first person to have made an open-water swim of note was Hinepoupou who swam from Kapiti Island to Rangitoto (D'Urville Island) after being abandoned there by her unfaithful and mean husband in the mid-eighteenth century.

Ditched, alone, upset and feeling the need to be with her whanau, Hinepoupou bravely decided to swim to the South Island, the home of her tribe (Ngati Kuia). She knew that her own strength would not carry her so far so, hoping that the sea gods would come to her aid, she chanted an ancient ancestral prayer, asking for help and strength. Hinepoupou then plunged into the sea and swam strongly. Just as she started to become weary, Kaikaiawaro, a dolphin, appeared and with this sea guardian's assistance she safely crossed Cook Strait in three days. (Some say Pelorus Jack was an incarnation of Kaikaiawaro. Pelorus Jack met boats at the entrance to Pelorus Sound from 1888 until the early 1900s. Jack was the first dolphin in the world to be protected by law.)

In 1990, six former Cook Strait swimming champions retraced the likely course of Hinepoupou's epic swim as a relay. It took four days for the team to complete the swim, and a plaque commemorating their swim sits in a rock at the northern end of Maclean Park at Paraparaumu Beach.

# BARRIE DEVENPORT 1935–2010

*First to successfully swim the strait*

Imagine being the first person in recent times to cross one of the world's most challenging stretches of water and for your efforts being gifted a truckload of manure. Only in New Zealand!

At the age of 27, Barrie Devenport on 20 November 1962 success-fully crossed the strait from north to south (just three months after the country's first roll-on-roll-off car- and rail-ferry crossing between Wellington and Picton on 11 August), battling a sudden tide shift and the diesel fumes from one of the support boats.

His swim, fuelled by a mix of orange juice and Complan sipped from a baby bottle, took 11 hours and 20 minutes. When you think about it that's like a third slower than a modern-day Cook Strait ferry—without the queues at the uploading.

Devenport and his support team had one failed attempt eight months earlier, and given that the Cook Strait is known for its notoriously complex tides and as one of the windiest parts of the country, it really is quite remarkable that anyone would try such a feat again. Although Barrie was a powerful rugby forward, he hadn't quite had the required fitness level on his first attempt. He spent the freezing winter months swimming around and about Wellington harbour building up

Barrie Devenport (waving), looking remarkably perky for someone who has just swum the Cook Strait with his final pacers Ian Greenwood and Jim Cornish

his endurance (and probably making most Wellingtonians think he was mad entering that chilly water). The turning point in his training was when he approached legendary coach Arthur Lydiard (see page 105), who said that Devenport wasn't aerobically or mentally fit enough for the challenge, and set him to running 10–15 kilometres a day.

As he swam the 26 kilometres from Cape Terawhiti in the North Island to Wellington Rock in the South Island, the nation held its breath, with Prime Minister Holyoake even interrupting Caucus to hear the radio broadcast of the result. The nation rewarded him with a civic reception the following day, and Devenport was presented with a new television and some thoughtful person gifted him a truckload of manure for his garden. Surely a pat on the back might have done?

Barrie's blue togs and the baby bottle are on display at the Museum of Wellington City and Sea.

In 13 hours and 36 minutes John van Leeuwen was the first to swim the other, tougher strait, Foveaux Strait, on 7 February 1963. Foveaux Strait is the body of water between the South and Stewart islands, and would have been particularly chilly—even in February.

The first person to swim 40.2 kilometres across Lake Taupo was Margaret Sweeney on 30 January 1955. It took the Aucklander 13 hours and 29 minutes. The friendly staff at the Taupo i-Site can direct you to the lakefront seat that commemorates this impressive Kiwi first.

## AMPHIBIOUS

On 7 January 1796, the schooner *Providence*, the first sailing ship built in New Zealand, left Dusky Sound with the crew of the abandoned *Endeavour*. Just over two hundred years later, businessman and Kiwi innovator Alan Gibbs invented the world's first high-speed amphibious sports vehicle able to travel on water as well as land. And, in a nice twist on history, British multi-millionaire Sir Richard Branson drove the Aquada across the English Channel in 2004.

# JOHN BALMER 1833–52

*First recorded shark attack fatality*

The first recorded shark attack fatality in New Zealand occurred twelve years to the day since the arrival of the *Aurora*, the first of the New Zealand Company's immigrant ships, in Wellington's Port Nicholson in 1840. Wellingtonians always enjoy a chance to party, and the first anniversary of this arrival had also been the occasion of the first rowing races and the first race meeting in New Zealand.

Twenty-two January 1852 was a sunny summery anniversary day— and the band of the 65th Regiment had performed for the crowds; whale and shipping boats lay at anchor in the harbour and all on the horizon looked clear, glistening and calm—below the horizon was a different matter.

Game for an invigorating dip after their 'musical labours of the day', half a dozen band members of the 65th decided to swim to the ships, striking out from the Te Aro shore and racing each other. One athletic swimmer, who was used to covering considerable distances, was the clear leader, and as the others gave up the race and headed back to shore, nineteen-year-old Johnny Balmer continued enjoying the refreshing Wellington waters. Also enjoying the waters, and probably the scraps of offal from the whaling vessels in the harbour, was a 4-metre long shark.

A newspaper report on 7 February stated that Balmer was bitten on the thick part of the thigh and the calf by the 'enormous shark' and that a rowboat 20 yards distant had tried to help but, although the rower managed to get Balmer out of the water, the boy died within minutes. A journalistic article written 43 years later gives a more dramatic version of events:

There within thirty yards rose from the water the dorsal fin of an immense shark . . . [the rower] redoubled his efforts to reach the swimmer . . . but was terrified to see him disappear beneath the water, pulled down by the voracious monster . . . he reached the surface and was again striking out vigorously [towards the boat] . . . He had got within twenty feet . . . when a swirl of that horrible tail above the water . . . the bright handsome youth was again lost to sight as completely as if he had never been there, but the sudden crimsoning of the sea told a fearful tale of the tragedy that was being enacted beneath.

Again he rose to the surface . . . he had once more freed himself from those cruel lancet-lined jaws, and grasping the gunwale, scrambled on board . . . All the vitality of which he was apparently possessed had been expended in the last supreme exertion, and lying down, in less than five minutes every drop of life's precious elixir had left his veins, and he was dead.

Though barely having attained the full age of manhood, he was truly a fine specimen of a British soldier.

A general resolve was then made to endeavour to destroy the monster, it was caught once or twice, but either hook or line, in each instance, proved unequal to the task . . . but no sooner was the sinister looking head brought to the surface and the harpoon poised to give the finishing stroke . . . the enormous fish shot away with lightening speed . . . and the unconquerable shark was free again.

Judging by the length of the boat which it had been alongside . . . the monster was estimated at from twenty to twenty-four feet in length . . . this terrible scare to bathers was not seen again.

I could say something about New Zealand journalism here, but I might offend someone who likes purple prose.

John Balmer was buried at the Bolton Street cemetery; you can find his gravestone there, just off the Chapel Walk near a giant pohutukawa next to the sexton's cottage and chapel.

The inscription reads:

Sacred to the memory of John BALMER, of the Band of H. M. 65th Regt, aged 19 years and 6 months. His death was caused by the bite of a shark when bathing in Lambton Harbour on the 22nd day of January 1852. 'Thou mourner dry that thoughtless tear, and gaze upon the dead, tis but a bier: no' earthly spirit lingers there, on Wings of light to heaven tis fled! This tablet is erected by his comrades of the Band as a last tribute of respect to one who was much esteemed by them.

# BILL HAMILTON 1899–1978

*First to motor upstream*

While everything that goes up must come down, Bill Hamilton believed that what went downstream should be able to go upstream.

For someone destined to make the history books, it's rather ironic that William Hamilton hated studying history in school. Actually, young Bill was kept out of school until he was seven years of age, as his parents believed that roaming free on the big-sky country of the 45,000 hectare sheep station in South Canterbury was more likely to promote a love of learning than the strictures and structures of a classroom.

He spent hours drifting down the local streams in a galvanised washtub powered by a couple of wooden paddles. Progressing slightly, his next vessel, a sailing raft of 5-gallon drums strapped together, was heavy and cumbersome.

Bill then made a bamboo and calico canoe which he navigated down the flooded Opuha River; the canoe was lightweight, but in order to get the vessel upstream again, he crafted a homemade canoe trailer from old bicycle wheels and coerced the family's retriever into helping. The dog was a bit reluctant, and the process required young Bill to leave the canoe downstream, run to get the dog and trailer, run back with them to the craft then lead the procession upstream again. There had to be another solution. Successful upstream travel was yet beyond his reach.

The retriever was retired from retrieving duties, and the trailer and canoe together morphed into a land yacht that sped along the rural roads of South Canterbury and marked the beginning of Hamilton's career as a speed demon.

Not the typical lazy teenager, by the age of thirteen, Bill Hamilton had built a dam and a waterwheel that powered a generator which may have been small but was big enough to provide the family home with electric light as well as power his small workshop with lathe and emery wheel. His harnessing of the power of water came two years before the first state-funded hydro-electrical station at Lake Coleridge in 1914.

He was sent to boarding school, and was frustrated that the only place within the establishment that he really enjoyed being—the woodworking workshop—was only available to him for one period a week. But Bill won over the school headmaster by fixing his bicycle and wristwatch. Unfortunate family circumstance meant that Bill's academic career was short-lived as he was required to help manage the farm.

In 1921, Bill Hamilton bought Irishman Creek Station in the Mackenzie Country for £16,000, and in 1923, on a visit to England, he met, fell in love with and married Peggy Wills. While there he bought an Isle of Man Sunbeam motor car—one of only four built in 1913. During the First World War, Peggy had worked in a munitions factory and had completed a dairy industry training course; her spirit of intellect and adventure was well matched to Bill and his New Zealand life.

The motor car, however, required tinkering with in order to satisfy Hamilton's need for speed, and Bill engaged the help of a local mechanic to increase the performance of the vehicle. Witnessing him hurtling around the roads at breakneck speeds, Mackenzie Country locals were none too pleased.

In 1925, Bill entered the Sunbeam in the New Zealand Motor Cup races at Muriwai, Auckland. He won the 50-mile race at an average speed of 81.5 miles per hour (131.2 kilometres per hour), and he achieved his first 'first' when he claimed the Australasian speed record and the first time the speed of 100 miles per hour was officially recorded in Australasia. Bill competed in many more races in the following few years and again broke the Australasian speed record, with 109.09 miles per hour (176.8 kilometres per hour) for the flying mile in 1928. In 1929, on another visit to England, Peggy bought a Bentley motor car and Bill promptly entered in a race alongside some big racing names of the day. Hamilton noted the track conditions at Brooklands in Surrey and worked with the suspension on his vehicle, ignoring mumbles and gibes from mechanics and other competitors who were tinkering with their engines. It must have been a real treat for the British to have an unknown man from the colonies win every race he entered—the first time that all three races on the one day had been won by the same driver. Yes, we're sure they slapped the Kiwi speedster on the back and said 'Jolly good show, old chap' as he took the coveted silver trophy back to this sheep farm at the bottom of the world.

Aside from becoming a familiar face amid a dust cloud trail to the local traffic officers, Bill Hamilton continued to innovate, devising ways to make the most of the power of dammed water on his property to heat his home and power his workshed. To build a dam he needed to find an efficient way to move earth, so he designed and built a new earth-scooping machine. The revolutionary scoop was so successful that he built a number of them to use on various contracts around the country—including helping build the nation's first aerodrome at The Hermitage at Mount Cook in 1935—and it kept his family and seventeen employees from feeling the pinch of the Great Depression.

During the war years, the workshop at Irishman Creek started to produce gun parts and bomb casings but the self-taught engineer's other tinkerings produced a water sprinkler, a hay lift, a shingle-loader, an air compressor, an air-conditioning plant, hydraulic pumps, a loader dozer and an ice-hockey rink with ice scraper smoother to make the most of the sparkly high country winter conditions.

With an egalitarian attitude and his mind always alert to solutions, Hamilton shared his knowledge and skills and urged his workers to do the same. He encouraged his profoundly deaf sister to overhaul the engine of her Bentley, and employed at his workshop some Jews who he had assisted to leave Germany before the war. The level of respect and trust from his workers was so great that he allowed the workshop to be by the workers after hours if they wanted to spend time on any personal projects. Hamilton was a man who saw things that needed to be done and created the circumstances to get them done without worry of what had gone before; perhaps this enabled him to achieve so many firsts.

What Bill Hamilton is mostly famous for is developing the jetboat, which is not a first but a commercial evolvement and a refinement of an idea of water propulsion. Before he did this, Hamilton was commissioned by New Zealand tourism pioneer Henry Rodolph Wigley to design and build New Zealand's first tow rope ski lift for Coronet Peak in 1947, thereby contributing to New Zealand's reputation as a ski tourism destination.

By 1945, Bill's industrious workshop had outgrown the Irishman Creek location and power source, and he opened up the C.W.F Hamilton & Co factory in Christchurch. Renowned for its work in hydraulics and finding streamlined engineering solutions, the firm took on many contracts including providing the intake gates for many of the hydro-electric plants as well as the chairlifts at Coronet Peak and the Queenstown Gondola.

If you've ever held a high-pressure water hose against a surface you will have noted the thrust of Newton's third law: every action has an equal and opposite reaction. Thus the concept of using the force of water to propel a vessel on the water became Bill Hamilton's new focus, as he returned to the problem of trying to get a boat to move upstream. Luckily, no retrievers were employed in this new boat-building venture where plywood boats were constructed and various engines tested. It was Bill's friend and employee Alf Dick who suggested that instead of directing jet streams of water below the river surface that perhaps the surface of the water would give more resistance and therefore thrust. Aside from trying to power a boat upstream against the force of a current, the other main challenge was the damage to propellers on stony riverbeds.

Of course, this is just what Bill Hamilton then started to perfect, and in 1954 he drove the first Hamilton Jet on the Ohau River. This first jetboat was a plywood boat, powered by a Ford car engine and the first upstream ride was at a sweet leisurely pace of only 17 kilometres per hour. But with persistence and painstaking development, the Hamilton Jet—the world's first propeller-less boat—and the jetboating tourism industry was born. The Hamilton waterjet draws water from beneath the hull, where it passes through a series of stages that increase the velocity of the waterflow, then expels it through a nozzle at the stern.

In 1959, Peggy and Bill travelled to the United States to make the first upstream passage of the 160-kilometre stretch of the Colorado River that runs through the Grand Canyon. And in 1977, Sir Edmund Hillary led a jetboat expedition in a Hamilton jetboat, from the mouth of the Ganges River to its source (see page 53).

Bill founded Hamilton Marine in 1958 and now Hamilton Jets are a mighty force on the motorboat scene, with Hamilton's refined technology being used for many high-speed vessels, including passenger ferries, rescue craft, patrol boats and offshore supply vessels. He was awarded a knighthood and is inducted into both the New Zealand Sports Hall of Fame and Business Hall of Fame.

Jetboats are highly manoeuvrable and can, from full speed, be reversed and brought to a stop within little more than their own length—making for a thrilling ride. It's difficult to imagine the New Zealand tourism industry without these adventurous boats zooming up our rivers, lakes and coastlines and through rocky tunnels.

Hamilton's invention doesn't just affect water-based tourism. With the invention of jetboats, access to remote tracks and hunting grounds has vastly improved. It's now easier to get to and maintain tracks, walkways and huts, which then also stimulates a greater interest in tramping and walking our national parks, and gives hunters an easier method of tracking in to remote spots.

## FIRST MOMENTS IN OUR RECENT HISTORY

The first hydro-electric station was built in 1887 for the Reefton gold mines, and this West Coast town was also the first in the southern hemisphere to get commercial power and electric street lighting in August 1888. Beating some suburbs of London and New York, it is known forevermore—to its residents at least—as 'the town of light'.

An article in the *Inangahua Times* of 6 August 1888 details the coming of electricity to Reefton:

A second public trial of the electric light system was made on Saturday evening last in Broadway. The night was fortunately very favorable for the display, and an immense crowd of people gathered in the street to witness the exhibition, and when, shortly before 8 p.m., the powerful light of the arc-lamp burst forth, like a flash of a mighty meteor, a murmur of admiration rose from the spectators, and there was an immediate skampering of feet towards the scene of the display. As on the former occasion, the light throbbed a good deal, but at its maximum brilliancy illuminated the town over a very wide area, with its cold, cheerless, phosphorescent rays. The

The bright lights, big city of Reefton, West Coast, c. 1888

illumination reached far up'on the mountains round the town, and gave a very sepulchral appearance to the hill-sides, the trees and stumps standing out in the strange pallid light, like so may tombstones. But if the arc-light was an attraction outside, the interior of the Oddfellow's Hall was infinitely more so. Rows of lamps were suspended down the building, encased in a variety of fantastically shaped shades of different colours, and the whole scene was one of striking splendor. It was indeed a 'Hall of dazzling light.' The lamps were all of one size, namely 16-candle power, but were not lighted up to their full normal strength, owing to the danger of surcharging the urgent with the powerful machinery, and so destroying the filaments.

# WILLIAM TRUBRIDGE 1980–

*First human to freedive to 100 metres unassisted*

On 12 December 2010, New Zealander William Trubridge dived into Dean's Blue Hole, the world's deepest blue hole, in a bay west of Clarence Town on Long Island in the Bahamas, and came back up, four minutes and ten seconds later, as a world first holder and record breaker.

What made 29-year-old Trubridge's achievement so extraordinary is that he reached the depth of 100 metres on a single breath of air and with only his hands and feet to propel him.

The next time you pass the State Insurance building in Wellington, or Auckland's Crowne Plaza, look upwards and imagine that much water above your head. One hundred metres is more than three times deeper than what's considered safe for recreational scuba divers, who must ascend from any significant depth at a slow pace to avoid developing air bubbles in the bloodstream, and the pressure at 100 metres is more than ten atmospheres (ten times the air pressure at the surface). At the 100-metre mark, Trubridge would have had 11 kilograms of pressure pressing down on him in the 202-metre deep hole.

Freedivers experience apnoea when the pressure causes their lungs to shrink to the size of a cricket ball and cease movement of the muscles of respiration.

Swimming an adapted form of breaststroke, he descended next to a vertical line, collected a tag from the bottom as proof of depth, before returning to the surface, becoming the first person ever to pass the barrier of 100 metres freediving completely unassisted—a discipline called 'constant weight, no fins' (CNF).

There are many different classes of freediving and in January 2011, Trubridge was awarded the World's Absolute Freediver Award (WAFA) naming him best all-round freediver. At the time of writing, he holds fifteen world records and he continues to extend the limits of this extreme sport.

In early 2012, he made a video that brings attention to the plight of the most diminutive of dolphins facing the threat of extinction, largely because of indiscriminate fishing methods and marine pollution. Trubridge is passionate about saving Hector's dolphins and filmed the video on the ocean floor, without aid of a breathing mask. Also an ambassador for Maui's dolphins, Trubridge, who tutors freediving breathing techniques, speaks these words underwater: 'We don't have long to fix this—saving this species is a race against time'.

Born in the UK, William learnt to swim at the age of eighteen months. His family moved to New Zealand when he was five and he was freediving to fifteen metres by the age of eight. He did not begin serious training for the sport until he was 23. William currently trains in Tenerife during the summer and Dean's Blue Hole in the winter.

## SHAUN QUINCEY 1985–

*First to row across the ditch, from Australia to New Zealand*

Shaun Quincey became the first solo person to row from Australia to New Zealand, swimming the last 300 metres to reach Northland's Ninety Mile Beach on 14 March 2010. The 25-year-old Shaun had left Coffs harbour on Australia's New South Wales coast 54 days earlier. During the 39,000-kilometre rowing feat, Shaun had broken two sets of oars and his boat, the *Tasman Trespasser*, had rolled a couple of times.

Although Shaun was the first to cross from Australia to New Zealand, he wasn't the first crazy Kiwi to row across the Tasman. That honour would go to Colin Quincey—Shaun's father—who 33 years earlier had rowed in the opposite direction, departing Northland's Hokianga harbour and arriving 63 days and seven hours later at Noosa, Queensland, on

10 April 1977. Colin had no GPS to guide him, no iPod to entertain or motivate him, and he navigated with a sextant, sang songs and solved maths equations while rowing across the Tasman Sea.

His advice to his son was, 'Plan, plan, plan and then give it your best shot.'

# 10

# OF BIRDS AND BEES AND DINOSAURS

## FIRST HONEY BEES

The sweetly named Mary Bumby is recorded as being the first person to introduce honey bees (*Apis mellifera*) to New Zealand on 13 March 1839. Mary was from Yorkshire and sailed to New Zealand with her brother John. Stopping off in Sydney on her six-month voyage to New Zealand, Mary purchased two straw beehives, the contents of which arrived safely when she disembarked at the Wesleyan mission station at Mangungu, Hokianga.

New Zealand has 28 native bee species (most of them black in colour), and although they do help in the pollination of kiwifruit and apple orchards as well as native flora, the introduced honey bee is the main honey producer.

In order to get one 500 gram jar of honey a hive of bees has to travel the equivalent of 88,000 kilometres—that's nearly 70,000 kilometres more than Mary Bumby had to travel to reach New Zealand shores.

In 2012 there were 420,000 beehives in New Zealand, although the varroa mite threatens to do damage to this population.

## FIRST DOG TRIALS

For far too long, world history books stated that in 1873 the world's first sheepdog trial was held at Bala in Wales, where there is a monument erected to mark that event. However, New Zealand records definitively record that Wanaka hosted dog trials on 18 April 1867 at Dog Match Flat, Cardrona Valley Road.

The *North Otago Times* of 30 April 1867 reported:

A trial of sheep dogs was held on the station of Messrs Holmes and Campbell, Wanak, . . . which was entered into with great spirit by the shepherds. We also observed a few of the fair sex present. The trial was only one of many which would be required to show a really good dog for all work, but as this is the first thing of the kind in the district, no doubt another year other trials will be added. The entries were numerous, and the running such as would disgrace no man or dog in any country . . . Each shepherd, with his dog, was required to drive three wild hill wethers, turned out of a yard, about quarter of a mile, put them in a yard of five hurdles, without a wing, and return them to the starting place within 30 minutes. The shepherd doing this best, and to the satisfaction of the judges, received a prize of £5, the second £3.

John Craig's dog, Sweep, came first at the world's first dog trials.

The article then went on to promote dog trials as a way of encouraging good shepherding:

On every run like the Wanaka—hilly, and in places rough—a shepherd, however good he may be, is comparatively useless on the hills without a thoroughly good and well-trained dog, on which he can place every dependance [sic]. If he has not such a dog, he runs great risk of either leaving a few sheep behind him on the hills when mustering and this will generally happen in the highest and roughest pieces of country, where they remain cut off from the rest of the flock, and probably escape the shearers' hands for a year or more, or if found in future musters they have such a weight of wool on that they cannot travel with the rest . . . we have matches and trials of almost every kind to encourage and perfect the breeding of other useful animals, while the sheep dog, one of the most useful, is totally neglected, or nearly so, by the majority of flockowners and shepherds . . . it would be greatly to the benefit of masters to see that their shepherds had really good animals to work with and to shepherds it would be a great advantage and ease to them to keep nothing but well-bred and carefully-trained dogs.

To celebrate this rewriting of history, in April 2012, a 2.7-metre-high steel statue of a shepherd and his dog was installed at the foot of the Mount Iron walking track in Wanaka.

There may be Welsh Border Collies, but the Welsh can no longer claim to have invented the dog trials. Wood engraving from the *Illustrated New Zealand News*, 3 September 1883

# RICHARD HENRY 1845–1929

*First eco warrior*

*First bird conservationist and caretaker of the
world's first island sanctuary for birds*

Long before the term 'eco-warrior' was coined, New Zealand's unique wild-scape, flightless bird population and evolution isolation helped shape someone who could be described as the world's first eco-warrior.

But this world first may not have come to be if Richard Treacy Henry hadn't failed to kill himself on 3 October 1893.

Richard's life wasn't all that happy in general. He had been born in Ireland in 1845 and emigrated with his family to Australia in 1851; sadly his mother and baby brother died on the voyage across the seas. In the new country, his father found it hard to find permanent work as a civil engineer and Richard's early life was rather itinerant, however, it did allow him to journey the land and get to terms with how nature worked. As a youth, he often went hunting in the bush, and on canoe trips up Victoria state's streams he observed the definite and varied ecosystems of dryland, swampland and deep forest, and talking with Aboriginal folk, he learned to understand how the diverse ecologies affected each other.

Richard's family suffered another tragedy when his brother was killed in a horrific accident at the sawmill which Richard owned with his father. Taking time off for a while to go bush after the accident,

Richard travelled to Australia's red interior before emigrating to New Zealand in 1874.

Richard spent the next few years doing a tiki-tour of the country, working at odd jobs such as hunting rabbits in an effort to rid them from Southland, and using his sawmilling experience to help with building a paddle-steamer on Lake Wakatipu, and becoming a bush-guide. There was plenty of work to do in the country, and plenty of country to see, but the raw beauty of Te Anau struck Richard and he settled there, building a small cottage by the lakeshore in 1883.

There he worked as a shepherd, explorer, guide, rabbiter, general handyman and, after watching, studying and then collecting birds, a taxidermist. His hobby turned into a fascination and he took to it with absolute diligence, in order to satisfy his extreme curiosity about the lives of the New Zealand birds that flew, pottered and scruffled around his home. To understand a bird's feeding habits, he would examine a dead creature's stomach contents, identifying which berries and bugs they had ingested.

Hearing the loud boom that New Zealanders all knew to be the kakapo's mating call, Richard noted the diminishing frequency with which this noise was heard in the night-time forest surrounding his lakeside home. This decline in numbers of the giant green parrot, as well as other native birds such as the kiwi, whio and weka, he correctly put down to the European introduction of stoats, weasels and ferrets. He was particularly taken by the kakapo, observing them and identifying that the birds did not mate every year, and was later to take the first known photograph of kakapo chicks. He wrote about the everyday lives of the birds, closely observing them in their natural habitat, come steady winter rain or glorious southern sunshine. Using his field observations, he prophesised that the bird would surely be extinct if something wasn't done about the invading hordes.

Henry started what can be thought of as a conservationist campaign, writing letters to newspapers and then addressing the public with his concerns in a series of columns and pamphlets. Finally his reasonings were starting to gain some traction with the Otago Acclimatisation Society who suggested that Resolution Island, the largest (uninhabited) island in New Zealand, be used as a sanctuary for flightless birds. In the 1870s, Dunedin naturalist Thomas Potts had first proposed the idea of island sanctuaries, but sometimes decisions by committee take far too long to implement. He had appealed for a haven for indigenous species at a time when predators were being introduced. The 208-kilometre square Resolution Island is separated from the mainland by Dusky Sound, and would be a place that few people would wander, meaning that there was less chance that stoats and weasels would also inhabit the island.

The island needed a government-appointed caretaker. However, like many bureaucratic processes, the decision on who should be appointed was long, drawn out and entirely disheartening for Henry, who any right-minded person would have realised was the perfect candidate for the job, given that he already had a broad knowledge of exactly what sort of habitats the birds would need as well as their peculiar habits.

Frustrated by the lack of action—or resolution—and suffering a deep depression after the sudden death of a close friend, 48-year-old Henry decided that his experience, knowledge and passion were fruitless if they weren't effectively endorsed by society. He felt useless and rejected and decided that the best course of action was to settle all his business, take himself off to a place unknown and see what would happen. Without saying goodbye to the Te Anau community, the self-taught naturalist left the beautiful southern lakes area and headed north to the big smoke of Auckland. In Auckland, Richard once again tried to get more advocates behind his campaign to save the kakapo, but was again brushed aside and told that trained scientists had things in hand.

Richard started to believe them—that he had no place as a naturalist—and, he therefore faced the idea of giving up the one thing that held him together. It was too much. So settling all his debts—down to his last shilling—ensuring that he wouldn't be identified, nor harm another, Henry walked to an Auckland bridge, took out a six-chambered revolver and shot himself.

The barrel was somewhat faulty, and the shot ineffectually fired and lodged a bullet into Richard's head, severing a nerve, but not producing the desired result. Determined, though now handicapped by a right hand that was unable to function without the nerves, Richard struggled to cock the trigger again. He felt his resolve to be clear, although it took him what he thought to be an eternity to point the cocked revolver to his head again. He pulled the trigger. And to his consternation the second cartridge misfired.

Before trying a third time, Richard was clear-headed enough to stop and think for a moment. Reflecting on the two failures he thought that, perhaps, it wasn't meant to be: 'the remnants of superstition made me think I had better put it off to see what would turn up'.

He walked himself and his still-loaded revolver to the Auckland hospital and admitted himself. Thankfully the attending doctor treated this unusual patient with respect; Richard described him as 'a young gentleman with a sympathetic manner worth a fortune'.

The newspapers ran an item with minimal details and the headline: 'Shot in the Head—a singular case—Second thoughts are best'. The papers described the man as being Robert Henry from Southland who had temporarily been affected by insomnia.

Reading this news, and recognising the description of Richard Henry, a friend sent him a kindly telegram seeking reassurance that Richard was okay. Richard replied that he was 'in the second best place' (the first being near his dear birds) and that 'I think I am all the better of it'. His friend replied and gave the good news that the government had now approved the Resolution Island project in its entirety but were still deciding on a caretaker.

His hopes buoyed, and grateful that this important project would now take place, Richard worried that his Auckland misadventure would not put him in a good light. He was keen to get back to the southern lakes again, and he returned there with new hope and determination.

But Richard was the man for the job—beating seven others—his application highlighting that he was accustomed to a solitary life, and was a good sailor, bushman and carpenter. And in 1894, Richard Henry was appointed caretaker of Resolution Island.

Richard's regard for the birdlife was immense, and it was this passion that drove him to transport 572 kiwi and kakapo to Resolution Island. Being flightless, and being on an island, Richard's feathered friends were unable to leave the sanctuary and he hoped it would mean that they would flourish away from all predators.

He built a small cottage and an iron boatshed and in six years rowed an estimated 700 flightless birds across to Resolution Island (distance 1.5 km return), in the hopes of evading the invaders. He pioneered capture techniques and recorded best-practice for releasing birds back into the wild.

Some years in Dusky Sound it rains 200 days out of 365. But this didn't affect Richard's resolve. He believed he was being useful and protecting the defenceless first inhabitants of New Zealand. Richard's heart must have broken when he first saw evidence of stoats on the island sanctuary around 1900. The stoats had swum the distance that Richard had rowed. He couldn't see a solution, and was devastated.

Although the world's first attempted translocation of birds to an island sanctuary could be considered unsuccessful—none of his beloved kakapo survived—Richard's hard work and ceaseless passion is to be praised. He can be described as our first eco-warrior.

After fourteen years on Resolution Island, he was transferred to the warmer climes of Kapiti Island where he was caretaker until he retired in 1911. He moved to the Bay of Plenty, then to Auckland where he died in 1929. Although he defended our nation's natural treasures, his legacy was not acknowledged at the time and only the Helensville postmaster attended Richard's funeral.

During the First World War the New Zealand Government requisitioned the iron off Richard's shed. Resolution Island was cleared of all introduced species in 2004 and is now one of New Zealand's offshore reserves.

In 1975, a male kakapo, captured in Fiordland, was the only remaining member of the species originating from the South Island, and was named 'Richard Henry'. He went on to sire many kakapo chicks but died in December 2010.

Richard's techniques, including the use of muzzled dogs to find kiwi and kakapo, are still used today by rangers and scientists. A breeding season in 2011 produced eleven chicks (eight females, three male), all of which survived, bringing the population to 131. However, several birds died and, with no breeding season in 2012, the population is down to 126.

# FIRST EXOTIC WILDLIFE

During his voyages in the 1770s, James Cook mentioned that the song of the native New Zealand birds was loud to the point of deafening, even when heard from offshore.

Nearly one hundred years later, after settlement had stripped native forests for pastoralisation of the land as well as for hunting for 'sport and science', the bird population was so diminished that there were large-scale insect infestations of Canterbury crops, and an insect-eating solution needed to be shipped in. On 10 January 1867, new members of the dawn chorus were first introduced when European bird species such as pheasants, partridges, blackbirds, thrushes, linnets, skylarks, chaffinches and starlings arrived into Lyttelton harbour.

# FIRST UNUSUAL ANIMALS

### Ostriches

The first ostriches (*Struthio camelus*) were imported from South Australia sometime in the early 1880s by John Thomas Matson to his farm at St Albans, Christchurch.

Obviously, ostriches weren't the only feather in Matson's cap; John's contributions to Canterbury society were highly praised by Sir Julius Vogel who, upon Matson's death in 1895, was moved to write: 'There are few indeed who have done so much towards developing this magnificent district of Canterbury as my friend, John Thomas Matson.'

And Silas Wagg—a regular 'comedietta' poet for the *Akaroa Mail* penned a nine-verse poem in praise of Matson, of which this is one:

*To rear the flocks, whose precious fleece turned*
*The life of arid want to comfort rare;*
*To breed the stately herds, whose products earned*
*Wealth for the Brave and splendour for the fair.*

Fans made from the feathers of his fine flock were gifted to Queen Victoria and Princess Alexandra of Wales. Matson also gifted a pair of breeding black swans to Christchurch and a handsome Kaiapoi woven rug to Te Whiti of Parihaka in 1894.

The first North Island site of ostrich farming is at Gittos Mission House, listed by the Historic Places Trust, in Kaiwaka.

Wealthy Danish entrepreneur Victor Nissen imported 57 birds from South Africa and then—after struggling with the ill-health of the birds and a drought—on-sold them to a farm in Whitford, though he maintained a position as ostrich manager. Nissen is estimated to have spent 'upwards of £12,000', which in these days is valued upwards of three million dollars.

Ostriches are the only bird in the world with two toes (yet still able to reach speeds of up to 60 kilometres per hour on the run—faster than any other two-legged animal), and their feathers were sought after in the early 1900s as the height of fashion.

*Hedgehogs*

Ever wonder why someone thought that snuffly, prickly hedgehogs would be a great addition to New Zealand? The little critters, who it is sometimes suggested are more numerous in New Zealand than their motherland of England, were first introduced in September 1869. The Canterbury Acclimatisation Society received a present of a pair of hedgehogs from the purser of the ship *Hydaspes*. An *Otago Daily Times* article in October 1869 states that 'While great things in the way of destroying grubs and other insects are expected from them, it is considered doubtful whether these advantages will not be counterbalanced by their destruction of eggs and young birds'.

Indeed, while most New Zealanders only see hedgehogs as an obstacle on the road or as a catfood-stealing nuisance, they are useful for devouring their favourite feast of the adult grass grub which annually can cause millions of dollars worth of damage to our pastures.

The hedgehog population wasn't terribly successful in breeding until the 1890s, and then they were deliberately distributed throughout the rest of the country. Mistrust of the prickly creatures still abounded—a 1912 article in the *Press* tried to counter accusations that hedgehogs had been on a rampage, apparently attacking and killing poultry and sucking the blood out of live chooks as well as milking cows at night.

The local museum curator, Mr Waite, was interviewed as he was an authority on animals, and explained that hedgehogs were armed with very small sharp teeth, and were thus unable to milk the cows' udders without leaving gruesome teeth marks.

> Asked whether the hedgehog had its uses, Mr Waite said it was quite common at Home for people to put hedgehogs in their kitchen to kill cockroaches . . . Mr Waite regarded the hedgehog as quite innocuous, but he was always open to learn that the animal might have changed its habits under the new environment.

It is now known that hedgehogs can spread disease between livestock and humans, though if it were a choice between hedgehogs and cockroaches, most New Zealanders would have no hesitation.

## BROWN TROUT

*First introduced catch*

Brown trout ova from Tasmania were introduced to New Zealand on 21 September 1867. The ova were reared in special covered ponds built in Hagley Park, next to the hospital, and the trout were successfully liberated into the rivers south of Christchurch and Otago. Salmon were introduced in 1868.

In the 1860s, angora and cashmere goats were imported, but by the mid-1870s they had yielded little economic benefit, and many had escaped and become a nuisance. Alpacas were also imported in the 1860s, but were decided to be more trouble than they were worth. The first zebra pedestrian crossing in New Zealand was introduced in Petone in 1938.

## NEW ZEALAND'S FIRST DOG BREEDS

Kuri were Polynesian dogs descended from the breed brought to New Zealand on the ancestral Maori canoes in the thirteenth century. Kuri were long-haired dogs about the size of a border collie with a small head, pricked ears, a powerful jaw and a bushy tail. They did not bark, but made a sound similar to the cry of a fox, described as a 'long, melancholy howl'. Between 10 and 15 kilograms, the kuri was a source of protein for early Maori settlers. It is not known exactly when kuri died out, but they were still roaming the country on Captain Cook's first visits.

If you've ever watched *Country Calendar* (the rural-focused television show which first aired in March 1966), or *A Dog's Life* (a dog-trials themed show which ran from 1977 to 1992), you will have noted that there are two ways that dogs herd sheep: the English sheepdog is known for its quiet, controlled stealth—working the sheep silently—but other dogs muster the sheep through various courses with loud barking. These barking dogs are known as huntaways, and although their breeding heritage isn't formally recorded, it is known that this New

Zealand-developed breed became familiar to farmers—and sheep—at around the turn of the twentieth century. British sheepdogs would have been used by early New Zealand farmers from 1867, and they mostly worked the hills and paddocks silently, but occasionally a dog would bark at the sheep, and the sheep would heed the bark. This barking trait was encouraged by some farmers who then bred these dogs with other not-so-quiet breeds such as the German shepherd, black Labrador and Border collie.

Regular events were held to test the mustering abilities of dog-handler teams, perhaps at the suggestion of the *North Otago Times* article (see page 201), and these events were advertised as 'hunt aways', thus the dog received its name and became a specialised herding dog.

The New Zealand huntaway is known to be an energetic dog, loyal and keen to work the hills and often mountainous terrain of the countryside. A dog handler communicates with the dog through a series of whistles and hand signals, and a good handler–dog team with a deep trust is a delight to watch as to the observer the interaction between them is uncannily subtle.

The small Rangitikei town of Hunterville (home of Christine Cole Catley, see page 91) has 441 residents and is well known for its statue of a huntaway. The highlight of the town festival held on the first Saturday after Labour Day is the 'Shepherds Shemozzle'—a race with person and dog—and shepherds travel from all over New Zealand to compete for the top prize. Farmers can buy a paving stone surrounding the base of the bronze sculpture to memorialise their own loyal huntaway's name and the dates of its working career.

## KATHLEEN MAISEY CURTIS, LATER LADY RIGG 1892–1994

*Mycologist and first New Zealand woman to gain an international doctorate*

*First New Zealander to have a native puffball fungi named after her*

An apple a day may keep the doctor away, but if it wasn't for one of New Zealand's first female doctorates, our apples may have long been blighted by ill-health and an unappetising appearance.

Before the first chance hedgerow seedling of a Braeburn apple grew in a Waiwero, Nelson, farm in 1952, the hero of New Zealand's apple and horticultural industry, and the international mycology and botany world, was Kathleen Curtis (later, Lady Rigg).

Born in the small Manawatu townlet of Foxton in 1892, Kathleen received her MA with first-class honours in botany in 1915 from Auckland University College, and then won a scholarship to study at Imperial College London (she also won the rather extravagant sounding Oriental Steam Navigation Company Scholarship for her fare to Britain), and attained her DSc in 1919. Although rather humble in subject matter, her thesis investigating the cause of wart disease in potatoes was considered the decade's most outstanding research in mycology (the study of fungi).

Kathleen was the first female scientist appointed to a research position in New Zealand when she took up employment at the Cawthron Institute—established in 1919 and now New Zealand's largest, independent research centre, based in Nelson.

She devoted her life to finding the cause and cure of many diseases that afflicted horticulture and forestry, including making contributions to the control of apple blackspot and brown rot of stonefruit.

Her highly esteemed research was acknowledged when she was made a fellow of the Royal Society of New Zealand in 1936. And her penchant for walking the hills of the Nelson region on the hunt for fungi was rewarded when she found a native puffball fungus that was later named after her—*Claustula fischeri curtis*.

After her retirement, and at the age of 74, Kathleen married her research colleague Dr Theodore Rigg—who had been the director of the Cawthron Institute and with whom Kathleen had been known to have a few intellectual battles; but they apparently played nicely in their marriage. Lady Kathleen Rigg—New Zealand's pioneer female botanist—died in 1994, having lived to the age of 102.

Although Kathleen is often cited as the first woman to receive a doctorate, there is another claimant.

## BELLA DYTES CROSS (LATER JENNINGS, LATER McCALLUM) 1885?-1927

*New Zealand's first female doctor of science to
graduate from a New Zealand university*

In 1919, Bella Cross presented her thesis on the economic importance of New Zealand flax, after having received a study scholarship in 1909–11. The gap between the scholarship and the thesis could be accounted for by the fact that in 1915 she married her first husband—also a science scholar, and a former New Zealand universities tennis champion— Lancelot Jennings, who became a captain in the First World War and was killed in action in 1916. Bella continued to study botany and also made some significant findings in the realm of mycology yet has not been particularly heralded by the history books, who seem to focus on her husbands' academic and athletic successes, despite the fact that Bella was also a high achiever in these fields.

## JOHN BUCHANAN 1819-98

*First person to record New Zealand grass growing*

The first person to really study New Zealand grass was previously employed as a wallpaper pattern designer. Perhaps watching grass grow is a better career option than watching the walls dry.

Born in Scotland in 1819, John Buchanan first worked as a foreman of a drawing workshop, creating botanical patterns for wallpaper and fabrics in Glasgow where his leisure pursuit was botanical drawing. He arrived in Port Chalmers in 1852 and worked as an assistant on provincial land and resource surveys.

In 1858, Buchanan was the first person to find gold in the Clutha River, and as he continued to prospect he also continued to draw and record the environment and flora he was observing. Under the wing of pre-eminent scientist James Hector, Buchanan's reputation as one of New Zealand's best scientific artists grew as he produced watercolour panoramas, detailed maps and botanical lithographs—his work was displayed in the 1865 New Zealand Exhibition.

Hector offered Buchanan a role at the first natural history museum, the Colonial Laboratory and Colonial Museum, which opened in 1865 to house the New Zealand Geological Society and the collection. The museum was one of the first government buildings to be constructed after Wellington had won the battle to be New Zealand's capital city.

During his tenure at the museum, Buchanan made many field trips covering the country from north to south, including the outer islands, and published over 30 scientific papers. His most significant work, however, was the indispensable three volume *Indigenous Grasses of New Zealand*—which illustrated the native grasses and highlighted their economic value for agricultural grazing.

In 1885, five years after the last volume was published, Buchanan returned to North East Valley, Dunedin, where he died in 1898.

## ETTIE ROUT 1877–1936

*First to broach the subject of the birds and the bees with First World War soldiers*

Born in Tasmania in 1877, Ettie moved with her family to Wellington when she was seven. Ettie started her own shorthand typing firm and campaigned for health issues, equal pay for women and labour issues (see Samuel Parnell page 287). She was a cyclist and vegetarian, and firmly advocated women's health.

When the First World War broke out, Ettie recruited a group of ten able-bodied female volunteers, named the Volunteer Sisters, and mobilised this corps to travel to Egypt to be nursing aides and workers at YMCA canteens.

Arriving in Egypt, Ettie saw the extent of the shameful secret of venereal disease among the New Zealand and Australian troops. The official estimates stated that perhaps 20 per cent of New Zealand troops had contracted sexually transmitted disease. The actual number was probably much higher.

In London and Gay Paris (where there were up to 70,000 street-walkers during the war years), during these early war years, groups of older women would walk the streets and pointedly intervene when they saw likely lasses carousing with soldiers, admonishing the soldier not to give in to temptation and setting the girl on her way home.

Matter-of-fact Ettie thought this avoidance technique ineffectual, and berated the 'nice well-meaning-motherly woman, half-angel-half-idiot, who specialises in "rescue work".' She knew there was a better way to prevent or at least diminish the problem of venereal disease and launched a letter-writing campaign to New Zealand MPs, newspapers, and health authorities. Her letters were banned from publication, and a newspaper could be fined £100 if they mentioned her name.

So, Ettie put together a kit that contained condoms and information letters and started handing them out to soldiers on leave. In 1918 the army finally relented and agreed to hand out the kits as part of the compulsory leave instructions issued to a soldier.

Knowing that advocating chastity was not the answer, Ettie then set up a 'clean' brothel in Paris where 10 per cent of Kiwi soldiers were bound for their leave. Soldiers arriving in Paris were greeted at the train station by Ettie, who gave them a kiss on the cheek and then provided them with a safe-sex kit which also included the business card of the brothel of Madame Yvonne where it was advised that all workers within the premises practised safe sex and were clear of venereal disease.

For her efforts she was respected by many servicemen; HG Wells referred to her as 'that unforgettable heroine', and a bishop in the House of Lords called Ettie 'the wickedest woman in England'.

The pragmatic and tireless campaigner knew that her actions would mean she was one of the most reviled people in her homeland, but she also believed in the huge societal benefit that her campaign would have. 'I stand with one foot on a hot brick and the other on a sheet of thin ice, so progress is rather slow,' she wrote.

In 1923 she published a book, *Safe Marriage*, which sold multiple editions in Britain, but was banned in New Zealand. Too many Kiwis had listened to what the British bishop had said, and when Ettie returned to New Zealand she was even shunned by her friends. Discouraged and upset by becoming a persona non grata despite all her good efforts, Ettie boarded a boat headed for Rarotonga and sent telegrams to her so-called friends. She then took an overdose of quinine and died at the age of 59. The telegrams read 'Ettie Rout died at sea'.

Ettie was buried in the graveyard of the London Missionary Society church (now the Cook Islands Christian Church) at Avarua.

In 1926 she'd written to her friend HG Wells, 'It's a mixed blessing to be born too soon.'

# JOAN WIFFEN 1922–2009

*First to discover that dinosaurs once roamed New Zealand*

Demonstrating that a delight in dinosaurs is not just the domain of six-year-olds, in 1975, a middle-aged New Zealand woman Joan Wiffen—a hobbyist geologist—found the first evidence that 65 million years ago, dinosaurs had roamed this land of the long white cloud.

Until Joan chanced upon a bone in a fossil-hunting expedition with her husband, it was thought that dinosaurs hadn't inhabited New Zealand due to the country's landmass mostly being underwater while they were around. Cretaceous marine reptiles were known to have existed in New Zealand's waters, but no land-living creatures. (In the late 1850s Thomas Hood Cockburn Hood had discovered the fossilised bones of a giant marine reptile, a plesiosaur, in the Waipara River, North Canterbury.)

Joan's discovery not only changed that view, but also gave the scientific world a reminder that despite little known facts, there were new things to be found if you took the time to look.

This remarkable discovery may not have happened but for a series of unremarkable 'what ifs'; when Joan was growing up her father's view was that education was wasted on girls, which meant she wasn't encouraged in secondary schooling. Young Joan had been fascinated by the shells she saw high in the Hawke's Bay limestone hills, but had been schooled to think that there was no future in study for her and she was expected to follow convention—get married and raise a family.

She did just that, after serving in the Women's Auxiliary Air Force during the Second World War. In the 1950s, Joan married Pont Wiffen and they settled into rural life together in the Hawke's Bay region bringing up two children. Joan would often get natural history books from the library for the children, and the family would go on outings with the local rock and mineral club. But the spark that led to Joan becoming New Zealand's most famed palaeontologist was when Pont—who had enrolled in a night course in geology—fell ill and was unable to attend the course. Not wanting to waste the tuition fees, Joan went in her husband's place and after attending a few classes found herself immensely jealous when someone in the class discovered a fossil shell hidden within a big chunk of mudstone. Joan realised she wanted to be a fossil hunter and became fascinated by the stories of the past to be found in geology.

Reading an old geological map, Joan and her family learnt that the riverbeds of the Te Hoe Valley, snug in the braided hills of north Hawke's Bay, had 'partly brackish water and contain reptilian remains'—it was an obvious starting point to hunt for fossils. Joan—unaware that the rest of the world thought it very unlikely that dinosaurs even existed in New Zealand—was on a mission to find dinosaur fossils.

However, this river location was remote—and making fossil casts and extracting rocks was a painstaking and difficult task as all the equipment had to be hauled in on foot. But the riverbed was indeed rich in fossils; Joan and her team found fish teeth, shark teeth, fish scales, vertebrae and shells, and over the years they discovered many marine reptile fossils. Joan was effectively teaching herself palaeontology on the spot—learning the skills of extracting fossils, scientifically recording and writing up the findings to send to experts for identification. She did all this on her own time and was unfunded. Then she found the first very significant fossil from a location at the Mangahouanga Stream.

Although she picked up the small bone fragment in 1975, Joan couldn't positively identify what it was until visiting a museum in Brisbane on a holiday to Australia in 1979. Noticing a familiar looking bone on the desk of the museum's palaeontologist, Ralph Molnar, she asked what it was.

Molnar replied that it was a tail vertebra of a dinosaur, and was surprised when Joan said that she had one at home that she had found virtually in her backyard.

Upon examination of the fossil weeks later, Molnar phoned Joan to confirm that she had indeed found a 65-million-year-old tail vertebra of a theropod dinosaur, believed to have been about 4 metres from nose to tail. This was not only extraordinary because it was New Zealand's first confirmed land-roaming dinosaur, but also because it was from a ferocious meat-eating theropod and carnivorous dinosaur finds are less common than those of herbivore dinosaurs.

So, despite being an amateur palaeontologist in a country that was not supposed to have any dinosaurs roaming its land ever, Joan Wiffen made a discovery that confirmed New Zealand did have terrestrial dinosaurs, and that they were probably the last of the dinosaurs to exist on the planet (over time dinosaurs were on the planet for 150 million years).

During the next few decades, along with her enthusiastic helpers, Joan Wiffen also found remains of ankylosaurs, armoured with spiky plates, evidence of huge plant-eating sauropods and small and quick ornithopods as well as remains of the flying pterosaur—this last being extraordinary as pterosaur bones are much more fragile and less likely to survive the processes of fossilisation.

Wiffen co-authored with Molnar some twelve scientific papers, and in 1994 the self-educated palaeontologist, who disproved accepted scientific theory, was awarded an honorary doctorate from Massy University. In 1995, she was made a CBE in honour of her discoveries and in 2004, she won the Morris Skinner Award from the Society of Vertebrate Palaeontology. She was affectionately known as the 'Dragon Lady' and died in 2009 at the age of 87. Many of her fossil finds are housed at GNS Science in Wellington.

Joan Wiffen put New Zealand on the dinosaur world map, and proved that there is still much unknown that is yet to be found. Scientists know that dinosaurs and ancient mammals lived alongside each other, and therefore if dinosaurs roamed Zealandia, then other prehistoric mammals were probably also here. We should take this driven, tenacious and resourceful woman's example and pursue our interests—who knows what we might find.

# 11

# FIRST ON THE CARDS: FIRST WORDS, LETTERS AND BETTERS

## FIRST TEXT IN TE REO/FIRST BOOK PRINTED IN NEW ZEALAND

William Colenso was born in 1811 in Cornwall, England. His first job after gaining his printing apprenticeship was with a printer who managed the Church Missionary Society's pamphlets, and Colenso was put forward as someone who would be of the right temperament (conservative and Christian) and the right age (23 years old with no wife and family to drag across the world with him) to be capable of running a small printing press at Paihia in the Bay of Islands at the bottom of the world.

He sailed to Sydney and then onward to New Zealand, with the schooner *Blackbird* limping into Paihia harbour at 10 p.m. on 30 December 1834 after 21 days—and many leaks—at sea. The following day, the immensely heavy iron Stanhope printing press that Colenso had been given care of—disassembled into a mass of mechanical parts—was ferried to shore along with the hefty boxes of type. Upon unpacking the press and trying to assemble its counterweighted mechanical workings, it was discovered that some important tools and parts were missing. Nonetheless, with some ingenuity and aid from the Maori lads who were helping Colenso as well as some DIY attitude, the press was made functional (it took another 18 months for the proper parts to be shipped from England). Another oversight was the fact that the Church Missionary Society

A plan for the first cases for printer's type made at Kororareka in 1835 to the order of William Colenso

had failed to pack any paper for printing, however, Colenso attained some from the local store and was responsible for the first book printed in New Zealand—a sixteen-page translation of a chapter of the Bible into Maori on 17 February 1835—and for the first printing of the New Testament in Maori. Translated then as Te Kawenata Hou, its 356 pages came off the press in December 1837 and had a print run of a staggering 5000 copies. Considering all the work that the man and the machine must have had to do—aligning all the type into cases per page, rolling the cased type into the machine, preparing the ink, and hanging the freshly printed sheets up to dry in the humidity of Northland—it was an immense task.

It was a significant event for the Maori people, whose language up to this point had been recorded orally, and the hunger for seeing their language in printed form was high.

The first English-language pamphlet produced in October 1835 was a warning to the settlers of the imperialist threat of Frenchman Baron Charles de Thierry. By 1840, Colenso had produced more than 74,000 copies of various books and pamphlets and teaching aides for schools.

William Colenso attended the initial signing of the Treaty of Waitangi on 17 February 1840 and was responsible for printing the first Treaty document. Rather famously, he raised the issue of whether the contents of the Treaty were fully understood by Maori and he wrote what is considered to be the best contemporary eyewitness account of the historic event. This authentic and genuine history was published in 1890.

Colenso arranged a marriage with Elizabeth Fairburn, the daughter of missionaries. For Elizabeth it was not love at first sight, but Colenso's union with this Christian woman who had been brought up amid the Maori people and was therefore fluent in te reo and tikanga was seen to be extremely beneficial to his work.

Elizabeth Colenso's influence as a teacher and scholar of Maori on the work of Colenso is largely unrecorded. Their marriage was not the happiest and it did not last long, but while Colenso's reputation as a fair-minded missionary suffered at his own hands, Elizabeth went back to England, met the Queen, acted as a translator for a group of Maori who were visiting Queen Victoria, was the editor and proofreader of the first complete Bible in Maori in 1868 and eventually returned to New Zealand to teach Maori girls.

The first attempt at compiling a Maori dictionary was published in 1844; the missionary editor was William Williams, of whom it was said, 'the Maori language flowed fluently without him seeming to ever have learned it'.

## FIRST MAORI-LANGUAGE COMPUTER OPERATING SYSTEMS

On 29 November 2005 in a collaboration between Microsoft, the Maori Language Commission (Te Taura Whiri i te Reo Maori) and Waikato University, Maori-language versions of the Windows operating system and Microsoft Office were released. A Maori-language Google interface was launched in 2008.

## FIRST NEWSPAPERS

The *New Zealand Gazette* was New Zealand's first newspaper, published on 21 August 1839 in London, sponsored by the New Zealand Company, and with a revision issued a fortnight later. The second issue was published in Wellington on 18 April 1840, making it the first newspaper printed in New Zealand. Newspapers were mostly text with the *Otago Witness* the first New Zealand newspaper to publish photographs in 1901.

The nation's second paper was the *Bay of Islands Gazette* published by Englishman Barzillai Quaife in 1840, however, the views expressed within the paper were pro-Maori and criticised wholesale land sales, and the newspaper didn't last long. The first Maori-language newspaper, *Ko te Karere o Nui Tireni*, was published in 1842.

The first daily newspaper, the *Otago Daily Times* came into being on 15 November 1861. The newspaper's first editor Julius Vogel was later to become New Zealand's first Jewish premier, and could convey his strong opinions with persuasiveness and flair. In 1889—after having returned to England—Vogel wrote a utopian novel (also see Macmillan Brown page 242) that uncannily predicted women would hold the senior positions in government by the turn of the millennium. *Anno Domini 2000; or, woman's destiny* is all the more remarkable because it was published four years before women gained the vote in 1893 and by the time New Zealand was the 'first to see the light' in the year 2000, we had a female prime minister (Helen Clark, the first elected female prime minister), a female leader of opposition (Jenny Shipley, the first female prime minister), as well as women in the posts of attorney-general, chief justice, governor-general designate, and New Zealand's largest company (Telecom) also had a female CEO.

Vogel's prescient novel also foresaw universal air travel (four years before Richard Pearse's first flight, see page 7) in lightweight 'air-cruisers'; communication through desktop 'noiseless telegraph' (think texts and emails) that journalists could use to basically upload news; and that aside from having strong tourism, fishing and agricultural industries, New Zealand in the new millennium would produce world-class wine. In Vogel's utopia, hydro-electricity powers homes and state housing is available to all with 'remarkable contrivances' replacing manual labour.

Vogel predicted that our industry would have significant impact on the environment and he got much of the future—our present—right.

Modern readers may find *Anno Domini* a touch slow-paced, despite its Bond-like hero, but Julius Vogel's novel—regarded as New Zealand's first science fiction book—was re-issued in 2001 by the University of Hawaii Press. Every year, New Zealand science fiction, fantasy and horror writers compete for the Sir Julius Vogel Award.

To try to meet the daily demand for vast quantities of paper, New Zealand's first papermill was opened by Edward McGlashan in Dunedin's Leith Valley in 1876. It produced true pulp reading material as the 'paper' fibre was made from combinations of waste paper, rags, old shipping rope, used sacks, flax and even tussock grass.

# SIR DAVID LOW 1891–1963

*The first (and possibly only) Kiwi to really get on Hitler's wick and featuring at number five on the list of the people Hitler wanted dead if he conquered Britain*

Considered the greatest of twentieth-century political cartoonists, David Low was born in Dunedin and became preoccupied by comics when he found a pile of *Punch* magazines in a secondhand bookstore. After moving to Christchurch he was taken out of school when he was twelve as his parents believed he was in danger of over-studying. Low had the benefit of a liberal upbringing where the individual character of each member of the family was appreciated and developed. David's father taught his sons to smoke, creatively cuss, to bet at the races, and—importantly—he encouraged rigorous lively debate about a wide range of social issues.

Imitating the styles he found in the *Punch* magazines, and observing a caricaturist working in Cathedral Square, David had taught himself to draw. His skills were soon recognised when one of his political cartoons was accepted for publication in the Christchurch *Spectator* when he was just eleven years old; from that day on he became a jobbing cartoonist.

He submitted his drawings to the nation's newspapers, but already he was looking beyond New Zealand and sent his work to London, as well as regularly entering—and winning—a drawing competition in Australia's *New Idea* magazine.

A Kiwi doing well at home is one thing, but a Kiwi making good in 'the Homeland' is another. This newspaper billboard of December 20th announced David Low's success in 1919

The *Spectator* gave him a regular assignment to produce two cartoons a week, the Salvation Army commissioned him to draw anti-smoking and anti-gambling cartoons (an irony considering his father's life lessons), and he was also employed to provide occasional courtroom sketches for the New Zealand *Truth*.

He became staff political cartoonist at the *Canterbury Times*, but his liberal instincts meant that he refused to draw cartoons promoting compulsory military training, and in 1911, when he was twenty, he was asked to head over the ditch and work on the Sydney *Bulletin* to whom he had been regularly submitting his work.

During the war years the poor quality of newsprint meant that the cross-hatching technique that Low and other cartoonists relied on made for a very blotchy newspaper. Low drastically rethought his style, using the pen less and taking up the brush more, lines became bolder and the importance of white space as a passive narrative device seemed to show that Low had drastically simplified his style. He had, in fact, honed it so that his technique and his biting wit were twice as strong and punchy.

His strong satirical style equipped him well for a position as the resident political cartoonist and he made a great job of capturing the large-nosed, small-man syndrome of Prime Minister William 'Billy' Hughes. A collection of Low's caricatures of the Australian PM were gathered together and published in *The Billy Book*, which was a roaring success prompting many guffaws from Australians at home and their soldiers abroad.

Ambitious and a dogged promoter of his work, Low sent a copy of his book to various newspapers in London and promptly got taken up by the *Star* where he was such a success that his cartoons were published by competing dailies.

In the late 1920s, he was brought on to the *Evening Standard* with the understanding that there would be no editorial meddling with his work. Low's cartoons were from there syndicated to over 200 papers and magazines worldwide during his 23-year tenure with the *Standard*. He developed a walrus-moustached stuffy character called Colonel Blimp who epitomised Conservative British reactionary attitudes and the sometimes absurd political pronouncements and complacency of the establishment. Being paid by Conservative newspapers to lambast the powers that be and the class system must have been quite an itchy thrill for Low with his politically looser socialist antipodean upbringing.

In his autobiography, he explained his Colonel Blimp character:

> Blimp was no enthusiast for democracy . . . His remedy to social unrest was less education, so that people could not read about slumps. An extreme isolationist, disliking foreigners (which included Jews, Irish, Scots, Welsh, and people from the Colonies and Dominions); a man of violence, approving war. He had no use for the League of Nations nor for international efforts to prevent wars. In particular he objected to any economic reorganization of world resources involving changes in the status quo.

Long before many acknowledged the threat of the situation, David Low's eye fell on the activities of European dictators, and it was as early as 1930 that he started to (literally) draw attention to Hitler's ambitions for a mightier Germany and domination over Europe, no matter the cost. It is important to note that in Britain at this point, some quarters admired the totalitarianism of the Nazi stance and actively promoted appeasement.

Low countered Hitler's self-propaganda by portraying him as a laughable little man with jumped-up ideas about his own importance. At first Adolf was said to have been flattered by the attention from Low's cartoons, even requesting a couple of them in the mistaken belief that Low's outsider's view of British politics was anti-democratic. However, as Low continued to mock Hitler by holding up a mirror to the man who'd like to be feared as a monster and revealing a not very flattering image of a pompous harmless fool, the Führer became more incensed.

Low said, 'I have learned from experience that, in the bluff and counterbluff of world politics, to draw a hostile war lord as a horrible monster is to play his game. What he doesn't like is being shown as a silly ass.'

Low hated Hitler and the feeling was definitely mutual. In 1937 the Nazis tried to put pressure on the British Government to restrain Low's satirical bite and the *Evening Standard* and any newspapers carrying Low's caricatures of the dictator were banned in Germany. This attempt at censorship only bolstered Low's determination to oppose Hitler and won the cartoonist more attention.

After the war, the extent to which the Kiwi got under the Führer's skin was made evident when it became public knowledge that Low was placed high on the list of people Hitler wanted to kill should an invasion of Britain take place.

David Low declined a knighthood in the 1930s, but accepted one in 1962, a year before he died at the age of 72. He'd produced over 14,000 drawings in his lifetime. Low once said, 'If you are ever asked to write my epitaph, you can say "Here lies a nuisance who was dedicated to sanity."' With a few choice words, and some understated Kiwi determination, David Low conveyed so much, helped bring the tyranny of political warfare to the world's attention and still kept his homeland close to heart.

The spectacle of Mussolini so masterfully beating up his Liberal and Socialist opponents was one that could not fail to evoke admiration in some Anglo-Saxon breasts. A British Fascist Party grew up overnight; and the *Daily Mail*, then Britain's biggest popular newspaper, approved it. With the zest I added the first Lord Rothermere, its proprietor, to my cast of cartoon characters. He made up well in a black shirt helping to stoke the fires of class hatred. Lord Rothermere was much incensed and complained bitterly. 'Dog doesn't eat dog. It isn't done,' said one of his Fleet Street men, as though he were giving me a moral adage instead of a thieves' [sic] wisecrack. 'You forget, old boy,' I replied, 'I'm a moa.'

*—Low's Autobiography*

## FIRST TO TEACH THE WORLD TO READ

Marie Clay achieved a number of 'firsts' in her lifetime; not only was she the first female academic in the education department at the University of Auckland (initially expected to provide and dish out the tea and biscuits at faculty meetings), becoming the first female professor at the university in 1975, she was also the first person to introduce reading recovery programmes to the world.

In 1948, after completing her MA hons, Marie was employed as an assistant psychologist for the New Zealand Department of Education. Her turning point in understanding education for children came when she was awarded a Fulbright Scholarship in 1950 to study developmental and clinical child psychology at the University of Minnesota.

Back in New Zealand, for her doctoral thesis, she investigated the weekly progress of one hundred children during their first year of school. From her research she developed and guided the implementation of a dedicated set of principles that became the reading recovery programme.

Clay realised that a one-size-fits-all literacy programme didn't necessarily work. Her first challenge was to teach as many children as possible to read well; to capture those who were having difficulties and give them one-on-one tuition was her second challenge.

Prior to Marie Clay's work, thousands of school children who hadn't been able to keep up with the class had been left behind and were set on a pattern of slow and repetitive failure.

Reading recovery is a short-term intervention for children who, in their first year of school, have the lowest achievement in literacy learning. It aims to prevent the downward spiral of failure that can often entrap children into a dislike of school and learning. It provides young minds with an intensive and one-on-one programme encouraging comprehension and development of learning strategies for 30 minutes a day for up to twenty weeks.

Before this time, the New Zealand social science sector was not awarded state funding; but the proof that her research, methodology, and reading recovery practice was extremely effective was very strong and a state-funded reading recovery programme was instituted in 1983.

In 1994, a reading recovery programme was given to 14,500 six-year-old New Zealanders. Within a year, 9000 of them had become independent readers and writers, 3400 achieved the same the following year and 1043 were referred to specialist coaching and development.

Her influence was not isolated to New Zealand (where English and Maori programmes are available), and spanned many geographic and language borders. Between its introduction to the United States in 1984 and the time of her death in 2007, reading recovery was used to help more than 1.6 million American children, and there was also a Spanish version taught in that country. It spread to Canada (with an associated French programme), Australia and Britain and Denmark.

Marie Clay's achievements in the fields of developmental psychology, educational psychology, and education were vast and earned her the respect and acclaim of her peers.

In 1982, Marie Clay was inducted into the International Reading Association's Reading Hall of Fame. She was elected an honorary fellow of the New Zealand Educational Institute and a fellow of the New Zealand Psychological Society. In 1987, Marie was made a dame in recognition of her service and successful leadership in literacy education, and, in 1995, Marie was made a fellow of the Royal Society of New Zealand.

Her book *Reading Recovery: Guidelines for Teachers in Training*, has sold over eight million copies worldwide.

## JOHN MACMILLAN BROWN 1845–1935

*First to nearly dupe the Nobels*

Although no New Zealand writer has yet won the Nobel Prize for Literature (though a few have deserved it), a Kiwi was the first to almost dupe the Nobel Prize committee which doesn't consider applications from those who nominate themselves for the prestigious award.

John Macmillan Brown was a university lecturer of literature, responsible for allowing women into degree classes on an equal basis as men at Canterbury College, the first university institution to do so. In 1875 he admitted Helen Connon to his lectures and she became the first woman to graduate with an MA in New Zealand and the first woman in the British Empire to receive an honours degree. She later married Macmillan Brown and became the first principal of Christchurch Girls' High School. Their daughter Millicent married Archibald Baxter, whose autobiography of his life as a conscientious objector, *We Will Not Cease*, is a classic of New Zealand literature and a significant recording of a part of history not often told. Millicent and Archibald's son was James K Baxter, one of New Zealand's finest and most revered poets.

After his retirement from university life, Macmillan Brown took to writing a number of non-fiction books on Pacific peoples, but these books and the views conveyed in them were strongly criticised by Maori scholars Apirana Ngata and Te Rangi Hiroa (Peter Buck, see page 113).

In 1905, John Macmillan Brown nominated a utopian novel *Limanora, the Island of Progress* by G Sweven for the Nobel Prize for Literature. However, it was later established that Godfrey Sweven was the nom de plume of Professor Macmillan Brown and therefore his self-nomination was null and void in the eyes of the committee. At 711 pages, *Limanora* was not the commercial or literary success that its author had hoped. You can still find copies of it at antiquarian booksellers.

John Macmillan Brown was a keen and astute investor and his name as benefactor lives on in the Macmillan Brown Prize for Poetry and the Macmillan Brown Lectures, and his bequest allowed the establishment of the Macmillan Brown Centre for Pacific Studies, and the Macmillan Brown Library building at the University of Canterbury.

# ROBERT BURCHFIELD 1923–2004

*First to sanction four-letter 'taboo' words in the* Oxford English Dictionary

*First New Zealand academic to critically acclaim*
*Tolkien's* The Fellowship of the Ring

You wouldn't think that a Whanganui-born lad would get to be the chief editor of the English-speaking world's authority on language, and be singularly responsible for the inclusion and correct recording of hundreds of thousands of words; but this is, indeed, the case. And writers, editors, word pedants, Scrabble enthusiasts and general lexicographic geeks of the world are thankful for Robert Burchfield's contribution to documentation of the English language.

Born into a working-class family in January 1923, Robert attended Wanganui Technical College, studied at Victoria University, served with the New Zealand artillery in the Second World War and then, as a Rhodes Scholar, attended Oxford University where he studied Medieval English literature under literary luminaries JRR Tolkien and CS Lewis.

Becoming a lecturer following his graduation, Robert was perfectly happy to study obscure Middle English and ancient Icelandic texts, until the college librarian—one of the original editors of the *Oxford English Dictionary* (OED)—recognised something in Burchfield and suggested that he help edit the OED's definitive supplement in 1957. Keeping in mind that the editorial department of the OED had been disbanded in 1933 after the last edition of the dictionary had been published, Burchfield was basically starting from scratch and building up the department, and the dictionary, as he went.

It was a task that required the accurate updating of the hundreds of thousands of old words already recorded in the dictionary as well as authoritatively recording the thousands of new words that had come into usage. How do you define words when you don't have a dictionary—this Herculean task was nothing short of phenomenally daunting. Oxford University Press envisaged that in a short seven years it would be possible to compile a single volume of around 13,000 pages. Robert took the job on, and 29 years later finished curating the 60,000 pages in four volumes.

Upon completing this accomplishment, which most editors would suffer a major series of conniptions over, he remarked to the *New York Times*, 'I took particular delight when we arrived at such words as "yo-yo" and "yuck". When we reached "zilch" and "zillionaire", it was like having the finishing tape in sight in a marathon run and we were entering the stadium.'

In 1972, Oxford University Press published the first volume (A–G) of the supplement to general acclaim. Within its pages were the four-letter words that previous dictionary editors were not allowed to include.

While compiling the supplement, Burchfield had the opportunity to consult with his former tutor on the etymology of the word 'hobbit', if it were to be included in the supplement. Tolkien had also worked as an assistant editor at the OED (1918–20), so he understood more than most the levity of Burchfield's responsibility. Tolkien responded that perhaps the best way to describe the word's origin was to preface it with the words 'In the tales of J.R.R. Tolkien'.

Burchfield listed Tolkien as one of his heroes, and after buying a first edition of Tolkien's *The Fellowship of the Ring* only two days after it was published, he promptly wrote to the author to convey his thoughts. He received a thank-you postcard, date *6 November 1954*:

> I am v. pleased that the first third of my large story pleases you, as it has not exactly commended itself to many of my other philological colleagues, some of whom regard it as a regrettable waste of time better spent on other stuff . . .

Between 1971 and 1984, Burchfield was the chief editor of all the Oxford English dictionaries, and among his publications was the *New Zealand Pocket Oxford Dictionary*, published in 1986. He remarked that every New Zealand word that he recorded in the supplement, 'received the kind of affection one would give to wife and children'. He felt a particular sense of Kiwi pride when adding the words 'pavlova' and 'pohutukawa'.

How many Kiwis would delight in being asked to co-author a report critiquing 'The Quality of Spoken English on BBC Radio'? So much to say! A lyric from the Mutton Birds could just about encompass what many of Burchfield's Kiwi contemporaries would have thought: 'the Queen's English is good enough for Jesus Christ, and it's good enough for me'.

Under Burchfield's editorship, a telephone hotline was established and it must have been quite a laugh when the editorial team fielded a call from a panicked New Zealand Scrabble player asking if the word 'vee' was a legitimate play (vee being the twenty-second letter of the alphabet, it was). But it also proved helpful to the blood-pressure levels of those of us who compulsively want to get the red pen out and adjust signage—one thoughtful signwriter phoned the hotline to confirm if 'accommodation' had two Ms.

Broad-minded, widely read and with a dedication to being descriptive rather than restrictive, Burchfield, with his Kiwi upbringing, certainly was more conscious of the need to include words that didn't hail from Ye Olde Englande and which were now a part of the larger English lexicon. Language is a living, ever-evolving organic creation and Robert Burchfield was insistent that the recording of the language was not censored, despite receiving a few death threats and being taken to court for a few inclusions.

He brought new words from new worlds, colloquialisms, scientific and technical terms all together and added them to the old. He also included the ancient, managing to get his love of Mediaeval English included; Burchfield put in examples taken from *The Ormulum*—a twelfth-century work of early Middle English verse, which is invaluable to philologists because it preserves details of English pronunciation existing just after the Norman conquest, when the language was in a state of flux.

In 2004, Robert Burchfield died of Parkinson's disease at the age of 81. He'd been appointed CBE in 1975, awarded an honorary doctor of literature by both Liverpool and Victoria universities, was President of the English Association, honoured with the Shakespeare Prize in 1994, and Whanganui, proud of his contribution to the pool of human knowledge, generously gave him the Freedom of the City in 1986.

## FIRST OPENING LINES

The first opening lines of a novel can either entice a reader to read further, or put them off entirely. In his quirky Gothic tragicomic melodrama of 1963, Ronald Hugh Morrieson wrote what is often cited as the greatest first line of a New Zealand novel:

The same week our fowls were stolen, Daphne Moran had her throat cut.

*—The Scarecrow*

According to the NZ On Screen website, Morrieson remains one of New Zealand's most filmed writers, despite writing only four books. Morrieson lived in the same house in Hawera for most of his life, working as a sometime dance-band musician. When he was 37, he decided that evenings were his best time to write, and he took on private music students. He won increasing fame after his death. Many Kiwis will know of his work through the 1985 film *Came a Hot Friday*—a movie that starred Billy T James (the first Maori comedian to star in his own television show and to be genuinely adored by the nation at large) which was a comedy of conmen, bookies and gamblers in a small Taranaki town. Morrieson died at age 50, a disappointed man whose cruelly prophetic words (see page 76) may have haunted him.

## ALEXANDER AITKEN 1895–

*First Kiwi to wrangle pi to 1000 decimal places*

Kiwis love pies, and we know to always blow on them, but one remarkable Kiwi is the first human to be able to recite pi to an astonishing 1000 decimal places.

The son of a Dunedin grocer, Alexander Aitken was born on 1 April 1895. He was certainly no fool but he was far from being a child prodigy and certainly was not a schoolboy maths scholar. In fact, he did poorly at maths until he was about fourteen years old, and then numbers became his prime focus. He diligently practised solving mathematical and algebraic problems and over time his numerical recall skills became evident.

While at Otago Boys' High School, he memorised the *Aeneid*, was the head boy in 1912 and taught himself how to play the violin. Aitken excelled in his final year of high school and achieved first place in the nationwide University Scholarship Examination, which meant he had a scholarship to Otago University where he started studying towards being a teacher, but his academic studies were interrupted by the First World War.

Enlisting in the New Zealand Expeditionary Force, Aitken served with the Otago infantry in Gallipoli, Egypt, and France, where he was severely wounded at the battle of the Somme. Throughout the horror of the time, Aitken provided some useful and light relief. His incredible recall came in handy when the platoon's log book was destroyed, and he was able to roll call the names and numbers of all the members of his platoon. He could also recite the numbers of his fellow soldiers' rifles and would play the viola to entertain his comrades. Aitken was sent back to New Zealand in 1917 after spending three months in a London hospital.

On return to New Zealand he started to write about his war experiences, but he let this sit for decades, finally revising the original draft. *Gallipoli to the Somme—Recollections of a New Zealand Infantryman* was published in 1963 by Oxford University Press. It was immediately recognised as an exact and rational account of the nightmare of war as well as a literary masterpiece and was described as 'an epic of devotion and sacrifice'. Before he'd left New Zealand, Aitken and the rest of the nation were led to believe that it was a war to end all wars.

I slid the rifle-sight to '450', aimed and fired . . . The Turk plunged into the trench in a swirl of dust . . . This, of course, was what I was there for, but it seemed no light matter, and kept me awake for some time. I would come to no conclusion except that individual guilt in an act of this kind is not absolved by collective duty nor lessened when pooled in collective responsibility . . . But I saw, still further, that this Turk, at the moment of shooting, had not even been a person; he might have been big game. It was a single step to the thought that certain 'colonial' campaigns, not infrequent in our annals, might have been conducted in almost this game-hunting spirit. Here I baulked; to become analytical might lead to doubt of the cause for which we were fighting . . . I was far from such doubt then, and would have repudiated pacifism.

Aitken resumed his university studies, where he achieved first-class honours in Latin and French and (ironically, only) second-class honours in mathematics. He married Mary Winifred Betts, a botany lecturer at Otago, and they had two children. He started his teaching career at his former high school, but then left to take up a scholarship at the University of Edinburgh. During his time as a teacher, he only had to look at the register once to remember all the names and middle initials of the 35 boys in his class.

Aitken wrote a PhD thesis on the 'smoothing of data', which was considered so remarkable that on the spot he was awarded a DSc and given a lecturing position in statistics and mathematical economics.

Aitken was soon recognised as an exceptional mind and, in a very British way, the *British Journal of Psychology* hailed Aitken's genius as exceeding 'that of any other person for whom precise authenticated records exist'.

Aitken helped develop key theories in econometrics, which is 'the application of mathematics and statistical methods to economic data'. He applied statistical methods to the theory of linear models and his generalised least squares estimator and the first matrix formulation of the linear regression model are of great value in econometrics. If that last sentence makes no sense to you, don't worry. Suffice to say that Aitken's academic work put economic theory into mathematical practice, and vice versa. Aitken's most influential statistical paper—'On the Estimation of Statistical Parameters'—was co-authored with fellow New Zealander Harold Silverstone.

As a lecturer, Aitken was a favourite with students; the first 40 minutes of a class were devoted to straight mathematics, then would come five minutes of jokes (have you ever heard a mathematician try to crack a joke?) and then five minutes of 'tricks', where Aitken would ask his students to give him numbers for which he would then write down the reciprocal, the square root, the cube root or other expression of the number. It was during his time in Edinburgh that he achieved the pi recall record.

In the 1920s, Aitken—heralded as the greatest living mathematician— was studied by the university psychology department, and asked to solve equations such as multiplying 987,654,321 by 123,456,789. Aitken took 30 seconds to come up with the correct answer: 121,932,631,112,635,269. And in under five seconds he could formulate a fraction to 26 decimal places.

In his late twenties, he reached great heights—literally—as he was a champion high-jumper. He continued to play the viola, and was given the accolade of being 'one of the finest amateur musicians'. He explained his technique for mental arithmetic as dividing numbers into groups of five and then making them waltz.

Aitken's extraordinary memory recall was a separate skill to his ability to understand numerical equations and, obviously obsessed with numbers, he would sometimes catch himself calculating the square root of the badges worn by bus conductors.

He was a speedreader and possessed of a photographic memory and an understanding of how to compute; but there can be too much of a good thing. Aitken's phenomenal memory recall was also the source of great and recurring bouts of depression that led to ill-health and eventually a breakdown. His memory kept calling him back to his wartime experiences and he was unable to forget the horrors he had witnessed at the crossing of the Somme and on landing at Gallipoli.

Aitken was elected to the Royal Society of Literature in 1964 after the publication of his memoirs. He was also elected to the Royal Society of London in 1936 for his work in statistics, algebra and numerical analysis. Undoubtedly one of the greatest mathematicians to be born and educated in New Zealand, he died in Edinburgh in 1967. The inaugural Aitken Prize was awarded in 1995 by the New Zealand Mathematical Society at a joint mathematics and statistics conference, held to remember Aitken a hundred years after his birth.

New Zealand was never far from his heart and in 1927 he wrote a poem (poetry being yet another string in Aitken's bow):

Through poplared Picardy,
One of the destined marching host,
I see by my comrade's side a ghost,
But his eyes are not on me.
And now for many a mile
Deep in the mazy forest gloom
I tread the blood-red rata bloom
In lonely Stewart Isle.
Ever the road beneath
Changes: now night begins to fall,
And I see the last long road of all,
The road to dusty death.

Here's what pi looks like at 1000 places:

3.1415926535897932384626433832795028841971693993751058209749445923078164062862089986280348253421170679821480865132823066470938446095505822317253594081284811174502841027019385211055596446229489549303819644288109756659334461284756482337867831652712019091456485669234603486104543266482133936072602491412737245870066063155881748815209209628292540917153643678925903600113305305488204665213841469519415116094330572703657595919530921861173819326117931051185480744623799627495673518857527248910

22793818301194912983367336244065664308602139494639522473719070217986094370277053921717629317675238467481846766940513200056812714526356082778577134275778960917363717872146844090122495343014654958537105079227968925892354201995611212902196086403441815981362977477130996051870721134999999837297804995105973173281609631859502445945534690830264252230825334468503526193118817101000313783875288658753320838142061717766914730359825349042875546873115956286388235378759375195778185778053217122680661300192787661119590921642019894

Blow on that!

# LESLIE COMRIE 1893–1950

*First to compute*

Many of us think that mathematical calculations are some form of wizardry requiring us simply to punch in numbers on our calculators and—bingo—the correct answer comes up. But before the electronic age, how were complex mathematical equations solved? Pukekohe-born mathematical guru Leslie Comrie had all the answers and was acknowledged worldwide as a pioneer of scientific computation.

Comrie attended Pukekohe High School and Auckland Grammar School, and studied at Auckland University College, graduating with an

MA honours in chemistry. As an undergraduate he founded the Auckland University College Astronomical Society.

Despite being severely deaf, Comrie went to France with the New Zealand Expeditionary Force during the First World War and lost a leg. While convalescing he began to use an early mechanical calculator and for the next fifteen years was obsessed with finding practical applications for punched-card machinery.

With a bit of Kiwi ingenuity and number-eight-wire philosophy, Comrie adapted a commercial cash register-like accounting machine to mechanically enable extremely complex astronomical calculations and thus automated astronomical and mathematical tables.

He studied at University College, London, and Cambridge University. He travelled to the USA to teach at Northwestern University from 1923 to 1925 and pioneered the teaching of numerical analysis (the methods for automatic calculation) in the USA.

At a 1924 meeting of the American Astronomical Society in Washington DC, Comrie gave a detailed survey of mathematical tables and calculating machines and concluded that multiplication and division could be achieved with calculating machines more conveniently than with logarithm tables.

In 1928, he was the first to use punched-card equipment for scientific calculations, computing the motion of the Moon between 1935 and the turn of the millennium.

Comrie worked at the Nautical Almanac Office, based in Greenwich, from 1925 to 1936. He initiated the first computing laboratory, and he revolutionised the computation of the much relied on, but very cumbersome, Nautical Almanac by using his calculating machines. In 1938 he founded in London the Scientific Computing Service—the first computing consultancy firm—which was to have a vast influence on the development of computing.

An egalitarian employer, he trained women as professional computers, teaching them how to perform various kinds of scientific computation with many types of calculating machines. And the mathematical tables that Comrie's firm published were said to be the most accurate tables ever produced.

In 1933, his friend and collaborator Wallace Eckert took Comrie's method to the next level by designing a control switch for his laboratory's calculation machines, and this automated series of complex calculations with a minimum of human handling was the basis of the new technology IBM computers.

As the Second World War approached, Comrie's bureau of computing consultants were increasingly in demand for accurate calculations of battle plans.

After the war, Comrie turned to commercial usage of his system and computerised British football pools. Comrie was elected a fellow of the Royal Society in 1950 and died, aged 57, later that year.

Comrie is also remembered for his work as an astronomer, having published many popular articles on practical (i.e. less mathematical) aspects of observing the universe around us. In honour of this, a lunar crater, 23.3N 112.7W, and an asteroid, 3521 Comrie, are named after him.

# GEOFFREY THOMAS ALLEY 1903–86

*First national librarian*

Geoff Alley may have found his first fame as an All Black in the late 1920s—playing as a lock in three tests and sixteen other international matches (including as a substitute for Cyril Brownlie, see page 76)—but what he considered his greatest accomplishment came a few decades later, and it may have surprised some who had admired his strength and big burly figure on the rugby field.

After growing up as part of the notable Cantabrian family interested in education and social reform (see his brother Rewi Alley, page 79), Geoff had considered becoming a priest, but ditched that idea and from 1929 to 1937 became a travelling tutor for the Workers' Education Association (WEA), bringing adult education and resources to back-country folk.

In 1937 he was chosen to lead the new Country Library Service, which he quickly built up, bringing books to schools and military camps throughout the country.

He created a system of recording the nationwide book holdings, which he had built up from scratch, and was appointed New Zealand's first national librarian at the National Library of New Zealand in 1964. He was the first All Black to be the hero of New Zealand's librarians.

Aside from touring with the national rugby team, Geoff also played for Southland and Canterbury provinces. But it was books that were his passion; he even penned his own—a book on the British rugby team's 1930 tour of New Zealand and, in later life, wrote articles for the *New Yorker* magazine. He also helped set up National Public Radio in Canada, where he lived for a while.

How many librarians you know can ruck like this? Geoffrey Thomas Alley: All Black and the National Librarian

## GEORGE JULIUS 1873–1946

*A Kiwi-educated Australian who developed the world's*
*first automatic betting machine in New Zealand*

Forget Nintendo or *World of Warcraft*, George Julius was the first to invent a large-scale, multi-user, real-time gaming system.

Although born in England, and eventually settling in Australia, George was raised and educated in New Zealand and was a graduate of Canterbury University. As a youth he'd been inclined towards mechanics and later developed the first mechanical ballot counter. He soon adapted it to become the first automatic totaliser machine designed to accurately calculate betting odds and eliminate trackside trickery. The first such commercial machine was installed at Ellerslie racecourse in 1913—and for that the Aussies loved him and knighted him a decade later. A totaliser is a machine that registers bets and in real time divides the total amount bet among those who win.

The machine at Ellerslie was housed in a building where punters wanting to place a bet could go to one of 30 booths and the machine would print a ticket out for each punter and keep a tally of the bets for each horse. The odds and tallies were then already mechanically calculated before the starting gun, whereas previously they had to be manually calculated and sometimes dodgy bookmakers could fiddle with the odds.

The first mechanical totalisor was put to the public test at the Easter meeting of the Auckland Racing Club, on 22 and 24 March 1913:

> Speculation was very brisk during the afternoon, with investments reaching to £41,514 10s, compared with £38,026 10s on the concluding day of last year, and making £74,053 for the meeting, against £68,947 10s in 1912, an increase of £5,105 10s.
>
> —*New Zealand Herald*, 25 March 1913

## POST MARKS AND STAMP-VENDING MACHINES

Back in the days before emails were the main form of communication, the postal service had a large part to play in the early days of the colony, so far removed from what some considered the civilised world. Newspapers recorded when mail ships would be arriving in port, and a weekly column called 'Philately' recorded anything to do with stamps and the mail—a useful resource for those interested in the way the world communicated.

## LETTER-STAMPING MACHINE

*First stamps on the go*

Born in 1829, and given a wonderfully evocative name, Fortunatus Evelyn Wright had to retire early from the Royal Navy after a not so fortunate bout of yellow fever left him with one leg shorter than the other.

The British descendant of French lords, he became a clerk in the Hong Kong Post Office in 1850 before arriving in Lyttelton in 1853. Fortunatus (or 'Forty') was the manager of Christchurch's first bank in 1856, and was the New Zealand Consul for Sweden and Norway. Significantly, Forty was government appointed as the first Canterbury postmaster, which was a significant position in the frontier town of nineteenth-century Christchurch.

In his time as a postmaster he invented a machine that stamped the date (of receipt to New Zealand shores) on envelopes. This seems to be New Zealand's pioneering postal invention, and one that was more effective than its British contemporaries which would only process envelopes containing just one sheet of paper—not at all practical for those long letters to and fro' the new colony:

Our readers who received letters from the Christchurch office by the last English mail will not fail, upon inspecting their envelopes, to admire the beautifully clear impression of the date stamp . . . Mr. Wright's machine have [sic] now stamped upwards of 150,000 letters, and the fine lines in the stamps appear as though they had but yesterday left the engravers . . .

In February the English mail was stamped by the machine, in the presence of Mr. Crawford, the Inspector of Post offices. The mail consisted of 5,524 letters, and was stamped by one person in one hour and forty-five minutes. Mr. Crawford, we learn, expressed himself highly pleased with the manner in which the work was performed by the machine . . .

The stamping of 1,000 letters was timed, and that number was passed through the machine in nine minutes thirty seconds. 300 letters were then stamped by the best date stamper in the office, and these took him seven minutes thirty seconds . . .

The stamping of an English mail is the severest test which can be applied to the machine, as the letters adhere very much together, from the length of time they have been tied up.

We consider the invention of a thoroughly practical machine of so useful and simple a character as the one invented by Mr. Wright as a matter of which not only he, but the whole colony, has some just reason to be proud; and we sincerely trust that his long and patient endeavours (for the invention has occupied his attention for nearly three years), may soon meet with a substantial reward.

—*Daily Southern Cross*, 6 June 1865

The father of eleven children, Wright was also a director of the New Brighton Tramway Company and a Justice of the peace. Forty was one of the commissioners of the oddly named Sweating Commission which investigated the low pay and miserable conditions that piece-workers, mostly women, were subjected to. It was the beginning of the Liberal period of government in New Zealand, and New Zealand can thank this man for being one of the first to promote the value of wide-open green spaces for the province that was to become the 'Garden City'. In 1873 he read a paper to the Philosophical Institute of Canterbury: 'On the desirability of dedicating to the people of New Zealand small areas of land assimilating in character to the village greens of England'. The *Evening Post* carried some of the text and then the matter was taken up by the newspapers and New Zealand society in general.

Many districts are now so much enclosed that a game of cricket can only be played in them on the sufferance of the owners of suitable paddocks . . . Were this idea [of village greens] carried out, the present and future generations of the youth inhabiting a great portion of this highly favoured country would have the opportunity of enjoying their hours for pastime with the exhilarating feeling of independence which would prove concomitant with the knowledge that the land on which they trod belonged to each and all of them.

*—Evening Post, 7 April 1873*

Fortunatus Evelyn Wright died in 1912 and was buried at Avonside Anglican cemetery.

In 1891 there were around 650 post-office workers, by 1911 there were four thousand more, thus showing the scale of significance that mail services had in New Zealand.

# WORLD'S FIRST STAMP-VENDING MACHINE

Up until the mid-nineteenth century, postage stamps worldwide had been printed in a sheet and then cut by hand. Perforation came in the 1880s, but it still took a New Zealand postal clerk to invent the world's first stamp-vending machine, allowing a one-penny stamp to be purchased at any hour of the day or night.

During his time selling stamps, Robert J Dickie considered tearing stamps of the same value by hand from a large sheet a rather inefficient use of time, and decided that a machine could do the job better. Like many creatives, Dickie had been turning his ideas for designing a machine around in his head for a long time—thirteen years, in fact.

'I kept banishing the idea from coming into being, but at last the urge would not let me sleep, and for peace of mind started working on the making of the model,' he said.

Eventually, inspired by seeing his first moving pictures, he started to construct the beautifully simple yet effective machine that was installed in June 1905 outside the Wellington Post Office. In its first two weeks of installation, the world's first stamp-vending machine had sold 3901 one-penny stamps. The machine won star honours at the 1909 Pacific Expo in Seattle and proved so useful and popular that the New Zealand Government bought the New Zealand manufacturing rights. Dickie sold the international rights and in 1938 visited an English factory where 800 workers were employed building machines from his design; 18,000 machines were installed in Britain.

His machines were in use for 50 years, only becoming outdated when the coinage changed. Robert died in Wellington in 1958.

## WORLD'S FIRST AIRMAIL STAMPS

Although we weren't the first country to take on airmail—only putting an official system up in the skies in 1921 (see page 3)—we can boast that we were the first to effectively have an airmail stamp.

When the SS *Wairarapa* was wrecked off the coast of Great Barrier Island in 1894, it took several days before the people on the mainland were alerted to the disaster and tragic loss of 121 lives. The island relied on the weekly visit of steamships to get their news and produce to and from the mainland. To provide a quicker means of communicating news and transmitting small messages, such as shopping lists, pigeons were enlisted, with the first pigeon post established in 1897.

Homing pigeons had been relied on to convey messages to and from shipping companies and were used by reporters to get trackside race results to the evening papers, but no regular service had ever been established.

The now highly prized triangular stamps of the pigeon-gram service are thought to be the first airmail stamps in the world. Aware of their philatelic importance, the Great Barrier pigeon-gram agency sent pigeon-gram stamps to the Duke of York and the Duke of Saxe-Coburg-Gotha for their philatelic collections.

The service lasted from 1897 until the first telegraph cable was laid between Great Barrier Island and Auckland in 1908. Originally a one-way service, the birds got to enjoy a steamship ride to the island before they had to fly the 92 kilometres back to their 'home' of Auckland—usually arriving less than two hours after take-off. But soon the flying posties were going hither and thither between island and city, carrying up to five messages. The messages were written on lightweight tissue paper, rolled up and placed in an aluminium capsule which was then attached to the leg of the pigeon. Reflecting the fact that it was more difficult to prompt a homing pigeon to leave its home than return, stamps were sixpence from the island to Auckland, but twelve pence (one shilling) the other way.

But how would the human postmasters know when these winged messengers arrived home? An amass bell was triggered by the pigeon as it entered its dovecote, and the ringing would alert the pigeon attendant to collect the message and allow the pigeon to rest and recuperate in the loft.

The fastest speed recorded between the island and the city was 50 minutes, a journey with an average speed of 125 kilometres per hour made by a true pigeon hero named Velocity. Certainly a speed not to be sneezed at—coo coo catchoo!

Bird fanciers will appreciate that, appropriately, there was also a pigeon-gram service for the Marotere Islands, in the Hen and Chickens group off the coast of Whangarei.

# A PIGEON-GRAM

On 11 July 1900 the Press Association reported:

A pigeon-gram was received to-night from Mr Philip Warren, of Port Fitzroy, Great Barrier, which says 'We have had a flood down here. The flat we had in cultivation is covered with, timber and stones. All the fences are gone. Everything on the flat was washed away—fowls, trees, tools, etc. You would not know the place if you saw it now. I think it must have been a water-spout burst over the place. We have not heard what damage our neighbours have had, but believe they must have suffered.

In 1903 the Mt Egmont Mountain Society would dispatch pigeons to the *Taranaki Herald* offices in order to inform climbers and walkers of the conditions on the mountain in summer.

# 12

# FIRST WRONGS

## MINNIE DEAN 1844–95

*First woman to be hanged*

On 12 August 1895, Williamina (Minnie) Dean, was marched to the gallows at Invercargill prison. Her death was the first—and last—time a woman was legally hanged in New Zealand but it wasn't the last the nation would hear of this enduring tale. Her conviction of infanticide remains controversial to this day.

Southland in the 1890s was a tough place for women who became pregnant with illegitimate children; with reliable contraception unavailable and the righteous society trying to pretend sexual relations didn't exist, many women either aborted unwanted pregnancies or the babies were abandoned at birth. Victorian attitudes (which lasted well into the middle of the following century) meant that young solo mothers were often rejected by their families and would have no 'decent' chances of doing well and getting married. The unfortunate girl would be sent out of town so the shame of the pregnancy wasn't brought on to a family, and then the baby—sometimes only a day old—would be passed on to a child carer.

With her husband, on their 22-acre estate known as The Larches in East Winton (31 kilometres from Invercargill), Minnie Dean established and advertised herself as someone who would care for such unwanted children, receiving either a weekly or a lump sum (around £10 a quarter). Taking in unwanted and illegitimate children for payment and procuring children for adoption was a secretive business that depended on discretion; childcare workers at that time were not required to keep written records, but it was believed that at any one time, Minnie was responsible for up to nine children.

New Zealand's infant mortality rate at the end of the nineteenth century was a significant problem and two babies who had died under Minnie's care in 1889 were ruled by a coroner's inquest as dying of natural causes and Minnie was not held responsible.

At the time there were English and Australian cases reported in the media of women killing their babies, and Minnie started to be eyed suspiciously by the community, some of whom said that children went missing in her care.

In early 1895, Minnie was seen boarding a train carrying a small baby and a hatbox, but observed leaving the same train with only the hatbox. Suspicions were aroused and the police were alerted. A woman came forward stating that she had handed over her granddaughter, only a few days old, to Minnie and identified clothes found at Minnie's house to be those of the child, but the child wasn't to be found and a search along the railway line found nothing of note.

Seeing a fresh patch of turned earth, the police dug up her flower garden and made the horrifying discovery of three bodies—two of babies, and one of a boy estimated to be three years old.

An inquest found that one child had died of suffocation and one had died from an overdose of laudanum (used to sedate children). The cause of death for the third child was not determined. Minnie Dean was charged with their murders.

Six children ranging from five weeks to fifteen years were in Minnie's care at the time of her arrest. The *Otago Daily Times* reported that the children 'seemed quite happy and contented. They do not appear to be very well provided with clothing but were strong and healthy looking, and seemed to have been well fed'. It stated that Minnie slept with the infant child in a room 7 feet 8 inches by 11 feet 4 inches and the five other children slept in a lean-to of 11 feet five inches by seven feet six and a half inches (that's about 2.2 metres by 3.1 metres). It was known that the Deans, whose house was situated 'in a rather lonely place, no other residence being nearer than half a mile and the Winton cemetery is within a few yards of the boundary of the Dean's section' were short of money.

Money, or lack thereof was an issue; one of the children, in Minnie's care for five years, had been handed over to her for a miserly one-off sum of £30. But despite these difficult financial circumstances, the papers stated that those who knew Mrs Dean said she appeared to always have an affectionate regard for the children in her care and that the children were educated to the appropriate level of religious knowledge.

At her trial, Dean's lawyer Alfred Hanlon argued that all the deaths were accidental, Minnie having administered laudanum while on the train so as to avoid disrupting other passengers. There were no recommended dosages, and the chemist who had provided Minnie Dean with the laudanum only made approximate amounts. The three-year-old was said to have accidentally drowned and the other child to have died of convulsions after having been given to Minnie as a sickly mite of only a few days. Hanlon contended the deaths had been covered up by Minnie to prevent the harmful gossip that she had previously been subjected to and which not only did damage to her means of livelihood, but also to the children within her care.

However, he was up against public sentiment with newspapers running daily headlines such as 'Baby Farm Murder Case', and 'The Winton Murder Sensation'. Hanlon later wrote: 'Sober, home-loving folk from end to end of the country shuddered . . . when the grim and ghastly story of Minnie Dean's infamy was narrated by the prosecution.'

The judge, JS Williams, told the jury that if they took Hanlon's contention as fact and accepted that the death of the child in Minnie Dean's care amounted to manslaughter only, it would be 'a weak-kneed compromise'.

Hanlon's skilful defence was admirable, but on 21 June 1895, Minnie was found guilty of murder and sentenced to death. It was the only one of more than sixteen murder trials in which Hanlon's client did not escape the hangman's noose.

Public hangings in New Zealand had been abolished. Nevertheless, the execution was more or less public as the walls around the prison yard (on the corner of Spey and Leven streets, now the Noel Leeming carpark) were not high enough to block out the scene from the surrounding buildings which were full of hundreds of spectators. While scrambling for the best view of the execution, a boy fell about 10 metres off a roof and fractured his skull.

Evening papers reported that the drop was 7 feet 9 inches (2.36 metres) and the scaffold used was one built for the execution of Captain Jarvey of Dunedin who had poisoned his wife 25 years earlier. Aware of how the public viewed her, Dean asked the attending surgeon to ensure they didn't keep her in agony; she retained her self-possession to the last and walked firmly to the scaffold. When asked, 'Do you wish to say anything before you leave this world?' she replied, 'No, except that I am innocent'. Her death was instantaneous. New Zealand abolished capital punishment and the death penalty in 1961.

Folklore has kept Minnie's name alive in the Southland area and she is the stuff of provincial urban legend; it is stated that no grass will grow on her grave and that if her name is said three times while standing in front of a mirror at 10 p.m. she'll appear. At Southland primary schools, apparitions of Minnie Dean holding a baby and a hatpin were reported and if you didn't eat your peas and cabbage a parent may threaten to send any fussy eaters to Minnie Dean's farm never to be heard from again, and naughty children are reprimanded with 'If you do that again, Minnie Dean will put you in a hatbox.'

Minnie Dean is buried in Winton, alongside her husband. Most graves face east to west, hers is north to south. Minnie Dean's tale still continues to provide intrigue; in January 2009 an official headstone paid for by Minnie's Scottish great-great nephew was to be laid where for 125 years none had before—the infamy of Winton's most famous resident previously having been discouraged.

However, just a few weeks before this official monument was unveiled, a mysterious headstone was placed on the grave (which does facilitate grass growing); it read: 'Minnie Dean is part of Winton's history/ Where she now lies is now no mystery.'

It sent Winton folk into a frenzy in the search for clues about who had placed this unofficial stone—to no avail. No one knew where the granite slab had come from and no one claimed responsibility. It was taken away and as no one claimed it was offered up to Southland museums. The official headstone unveiling and memorial service attracted a crowd of 100 or so, and the themes of peace, reconciliation and healing were emphasised when many of the crowd laid white flowers on Minnie's grave. In Victorian times white flowers symbolised forgiveness. Winton seems to have made peace with Minnie Dean, who while waiting for her time in the gallows wrote:

> The thought and hope of being able to see them only once has sustained me in all my bitter trouble. And surely I have been punished enough without inflicting the worst of all troubles on me. What is to become of them now? Who will love and care for them as I have done? Oh it is cruel to have to go to the grave with the only ray of comfort denied me, a fond last look at the faces of my little ones.

There's a biography and a recent novel based on Minnie's life, a country folk song and video about Minnie and an Emmy-nominated television series about Hanlon's illustrious career—one episode of which deals with the Minnie Dean case, and is available to view on the NZ On Screen website.

In the 1920s the conviction and subsequent hanging of a man in connection with 'baby farming' murders showed that the 'problem' of how to accommodate unwanted children was still rife.

## MAKETU WHARETOTARA 1824–42

*First to be hanged*

New Zealand's first case of a person hanged by the legal process also incorporated a number of other New Zealand firsts; British sovereignty had been established two years earlier and the murder trial—although not the first in New Zealand (that having occurred the day before)—was the first criminal sitting of the Supreme Court of New Zealand, and the conviction of murder was decided by the colony's first Chief Justice, Sir William Martin.

In November 1841, Maketu Wharetotara, the sixteen-year-old son of Nga Puhi chief, Ruhe of Waimate, worked as a farm labourer for widow Elizabeth Roberton in the Bay of Islands. Elizabeth's servant, Thomas Bull, bullied Maketu both physically and verbally, kicking the Maori lad, and on 18 November there was a vehement dispute about wage payment between the two. Two days later, Thomas, Elizabeth, her children and a young house girl (the granddaughter of Nga Puhi leader Rewa) were found dead. Maketu was the obvious culprit, and he fled.

Although Maketu sought refuge in his father's village, in order to avoid hostility or war with Rewa, Ruhe was forced to surrender his son to the government authorities. Allaying the European's fear of an impending bloody battle (after relative peace had just been attained following the Treaty of Waitangi signing), Ruhe and other Nga Puhi leaders issued a statement that Maketu's actions were his alone and they had no wish for war. Hone Heke, however, spoke out against handing over the Maori youth to the new system which he felt held no authority over the Maori people. This first major test of the application of British law to a Maori offender had to be handled with care.

The trial date was set, but—realising that in order to prove the over-arching idea of the objective impartiality and authority of the British judicial system—the case of a European man who was charged with the murder of a Maori woman, Rangihoua Kuika, was heard first. However, this man escaped the death penalty and was convicted of manslaughter. Maori later questioned this objectivity which seemed to have let the European murderer live despite strong evidence of his guilt.

As his opening address to the jury, Maketu's Crown-appointed lawyer, CB Brewer, outlined how little chance he'd had to prepare his case:

> May it please the Court—Gentlemen of the Jury, in rising to address you in defence of the unfortunate prisoner, I feel the importance of the duty that devolves upon me, and I deeply regret the very short period that I have had to prepare myself for it. I was only retained this morning, about an hour before the trial came on; I have had no opportunity of communicating with my client, nor did I see the depositions before I came into Court this morning . . .

He also maintained that the severity of the penalty, should Maketu be convicted of murder, was brutally heavy for one who was not aware of how the new laws of the land would affect him:

> This, Gentlemen, is the first case in which a New Zealander has been brought before our Courts, to be tried by our laws. Altho' the objection I took to the jurisdiction of the Court, on the ground of the prisoner's ignorance of the penal enactment of our law, and of his having no possible means or opportunity of understanding them, was overruled by the Court, still, I must insist that those circumstances ought to have some weight with you in the verdict which it is your duty to return.

Brewer stated that all the witnesses to the murders were dead and that the only evidence against Maketu was his own confessions.

His words translated by missionaries, Maketu pleaded not guilty and claimed that Thomas Bull and Mrs Roberton had offended his mana.

He was convicted, and hanged on 7 March 1842 at the corner of Queen and Victoria streets in Auckland. Maketu was originally buried in the old gaol grounds, but was later interred at a family burial ground in the Bay of Islands.

The *New Zealand Gazette* (New Zealand's first newspaper, see page 231) reported the hanging:

> The prisoner, (a fine young man) whose stature was upwards of six-feet, was brought from the condemned cell soon after 12 o'clock, to the platform . . . A strong, military guard had been drawn up in front of the gaol, where the scaffold was erected. A large square was left clear, on the four sides of which was assembled about a thousand spectators.

There seemed to be a general consensus by Maori of the time that although Maketu may have been guilty, the process of hanging was a needlessly slow and barbarously cold-blooded way to kill a man.

The New Zealand judicial system continued its brutal practice of hanging, and 115 years later Walter Bolton was the last person to be hanged for allegedly poisoning his wife, Beatrice. The Crown asserted that Bolton had put small amounts of arsenic (found in sheep dip) into her tea on a daily basis. Bolton maintained he was innocent until the last. The evidence around this Crown case was minimal, seeing as traces of arsenic were also found in Walter's blood, and it was due to the contentiousness of this case that the death penalty in New Zealand was abolished.

## FIRST EUROPEAN EXECUTED

Joseph Burns, a ship's carpenter for the British Navy, had arrived in the Bay of Islands in 1840; the vessel he was on made a rather dramatic entrance by wrecking at Mercury Bay.

Seven years later, Joseph was an odd-jobs man in Auckland with a chequered past involving heavy drinking, assault of his employer and stealing stock. In October 1847, Joseph was finding it difficult to keep jobs and support his partner Margaret Reardon and her children. In an attempt to steal £12 of wages, Burns murdered Robert Snow, a naval lieutenant, his wife and their daughter at their home in Devonport, Auckland. Aware that there were Maori camped in the area, Burns mutilated the bodies to suggest a Maori attack and burned the house knowing that the blame would likely fall on the Maori. He absconded to Australia for a few weeks, and returned to try to persuade his partner Margaret to marry him so that she would not be able to give evidence against him, should it come to that. When she refused, he brutally attacked her in a drunken rage and tried to end his own life. He was taken into police custody and sentenced to transportation for life. Burns coerced Margaret to corroborate his story that his fellow ex-shipmates, Thomas Duder and William Oliver, had committed the Snow murders. His story did not wash and he was charged with murder; at the trial he accused Margaret of prompting him to make a false confession and he took the opportunity to point out that Margaret had committed perjury.

The *New Zealander* reported that Burns 'remained relentless and impassive his mind a prey to one undying desire of vengeance on his miserable concubine, the chief instalment of his conviction, and whom he longed to render participatress of his punishment'. Poor Margaret confessed to perjury and confirmed that Joseph Burns was the murderer of the Snows.

Chief Justice William Martin declared Burns to be guilty and sentenced him to death. Burns was taken by police escort to the scene of his crime in Devonport and hanged on 17 June 1848 before a large crowd of settlers and Maori. He managed to make one last parting shot to Margaret, asking the attending religious minister to relay it for him:

> Burns desires me to say, as his last words, that the causes which have led him to this sad end, are indulgence in two sinful courses—his fondness for bad women, and his love of drinking. From these evil beginnings he dates his ruin.

Burns was the first European to be hanged in New Zealand under British law. Poor Margaret's punishment for having taken up with this awful man didn't end with his death; in September she was convicted of perjury and sentenced to seven years' transportation.

# 13

# BOUNDARY CREATORS AND RECORD MAKERS

## FIRST ELECTRIC FENCE

Joe started it. Joe had a fondness for cars, specifically scratching his large behind against the vehicle and managing to rock it with the sheer force of bad habit. Joe was a horse and Bill Gallagher set about trying to find a way to discourage this activity which had the potential to do damage to the family car.

Bill made a device that would electrify the outside of the parked car whenever it was rocked by attaching an ignition coil from his car to pieces from a Meccano set. Joe was a little shocked at this innovation, but soon got the message and didn't approach the vehicle again.

By 1937, Gallagher had expanded on his idea, seeing it would have great application in the New Zealand farming industry. So improving his cheap and permanent fencing solution, he took Gallagher Power Fencing—and the electric fence—to the world. Bill Gallagher used to test the 'kick' of the fencing system by holding both ends and this mad Kiwi dedication to the development and understanding of the product helped establish Gallagher Group Ltd as leaders in electric fencing systems, a position that they still hold today. The very Kiwi experience of incorrectly assuming an electric fence is switched off and the resulting snapping buzz after contact can all be traced back to one man, his horse and his car. Bill's invention was remembered with a New Zealand Post stamp in 2007. Joe does not feature on the 50 cent stamp.

## BAEYERTZ TAPE

*The first way to measure birth date*

Wanting to find an easy and accurate method of determining when a pregnant woman would give birth, Dr John Baeyertz found a non-intrusive way to establish a due date if the exact conception date was unknown.

The Whanganui obstetrician developed a measuring tape that when strapped across a pregnant belly could accurately measure how far along the pregnancy was and how long until birth. He used data from births where the exact date of conception was known—i.e. babies conceived by artificial insemination—and the patented technique proved very successful and is now used all around the world.

## FIRST TO PUT A LID ON IT

The next time you open up a tin of Milo, golden syrup or house paint, have a kind thought for John Eustace who invented the lipped airtight lid but whose idea was pilfered causing him to lose out on a fortune.

Eustace sent a working sample to England where he hoped a die would be cut so that he could easily mass-produce his innovation, but he was a little too trusting in the professionalism of others and hadn't taken out a worldwide patent, meaning that other people were legally able to copy his idea without paying our Kiwi inventor a cent. The Dunedin tinsmith continued what he had been doing, in the 1920s producing 100 tonnes of tin cans per year. He didn't make his fortune, though others made a profit from his simply effective and innovative idea.

## GEORGE VERNON HUDSON 1867–1946

*First to introduce daylight saving*

Sometimes great innovative ideas come from the most mundane aspects of the daily grind. And sometimes a recreational pursuit requires that little bit more time away from the office to be able to be thoroughly enjoyed.

The man who first introduced the idea of Daylight Saving to the world was a humble Wellington postal clerk for some hours of the day and evening, and in his spare daylight hours was a gentleman naturalist and lepidopterist, and an amateur astronomer in his spare evening hours.

As a self-taught naturalist and entomologist, Hudson found there weren't enough hours in the day to do the very thing he most enjoyed—observing terrestrial bodies of New Zealand's insects, butterflies and moths, or to record changes in extra-terrestrial bodies which he observed with his backyard telescope. It was his odd hours doing shift work that led George Hudson to think of the benefits of having extra sun-lit time in the summer months.

George Vernon Hudson was born in London and arrived in New Zealand when he was fourteen, by which age he had published a short paper in *The Entomologist*, exhibited a moth at a meeting of the Royal Entomological Society of London, and had observed and recorded an eclipse of the sun—certainly an accomplished teen.

George Vernon Hudson was a postal clerk who wanted more spare time and helped us all to see the light

New Zealand insect life provided George with plenty to observe and catalogue—his first scientific paper on New Zealand insects was published at the age of fifteen, at sixteen he started working for the Wellington Post Office and by eighteen he had joined the Wellington Philosophical Society, the forerunner to the Royal Society of New Zealand.

George had never been a fan of formal education—his school peers bullied him remorselessly for his unusual dedication to the insect world, so learning from the world and people—and bugs—around him was more to George's liking. His father—a stained-glass artist and craftsman—had passed on a love of fine detailed art, and George Hudson not only wrote about his six-legged friends, but also skilfully and elegantly illustrated them with fine brushstroke. When he was nineteen, he finished writing his first book—*An Elementary Manual of New Zealand Entomology* was published in 1892. He published six other books, including a three-volume treatise on butterflies and moths with over 2500 paintings of insects. He built a home for himself in the wilderness of the hills overlooking the emerging city of Wellington.

George (always impressively turned out in a three-piece suit) realised that more daylight hours would equate to more time to spend in the field scouring for and observing insects, and on 16 October 1895 he presented a paper to the Wellington Philosophical Society advocating what he termed seasonal time adjustment. He argued that the adjustment in time—surely an arbitrary notion anyway—would save energy by lessening the use of lights. The idea was originally ridiculed by many society members, and the public at large, so George returned to his suggestion at a further meeting in October 1898, clarifying some points of contention:

In this way the early-morning daylight would be utilised, and a long period of daylight leisure would be made available in the evening for cricket, gardening, cycling, or any other outdoor pursuit desired. It will no doubt be urged that people are at present quite at liberty to make use of the early-morning daylight in summer without any such drastic alteration in the established order of things as is here suggested. To this objection it may be pointed out that, living as we do in a social community, we are unable to separate ourselves from the habits of those around us. We cannot individually alter our times of going to bed or getting up, but must fall in with the habits of the majority—at all events, to a great extent. Again, under the present arrangement, those who desire to utilise the early-morning daylight are compelled to take some of their recreation before their daily work and some afterwards, which in many cases results in their having to forego pursuits that they would be enabled to follow successfully if their daylight leisure were continuous.

The phrase 'before its time' may be well used here; Hudson's proposal was still a controversial idea, but eventually, with the backing and advocacy of Thomas K Sidey, a Liberal MP from Dunedin, it gained acceptance and one hour summer time was trialled successfully in 1927. (New Zealand only adopted it after the United States and the UK had trialled it during the First World War and declared it a good way to save energy—and money—in the Depression years.)

George Hudson continued his astronomical studies and his Karori home was a gathering point for people to observe the 1910 transit of Halley's Comet. Where some blokes had sheds in their backyard, Hudson built himself an observatory and it was here, with the use of a four-inch telescope, that he was the first to observe a bright new star, Nova Aquilae, on 9 June 1918.

His discovery was reported worldwide with a press article that included a quote from the director of the Wanganui Observatory (a Mr M Ward) stating that some great stellar catastrophe must have taken place: 'It may be that a dark star crashed into a cloud of cosmic matter and thus generated an enormous outburst of light and heat. It is so far away that the catastrophe possibly happened hundreds of years ago.'

Hudson had moved up in the postal world and retired as the chief clerk in 1918. He was elected one of the original fellows of the New Zealand Institute in 1919, and was awarded the Hector Memorial Medal and Prize in 1923; he died in 1946.

Daylight Savings Time makes summer days longer, as well as a portion of spring and autumn days; it is of great economic benefit to the retail and tourism trades, but not so great for farmers. Kiwis should celebrate Hudson for giving us an extra hour a day to frolic, relax, go for a jog with the mountain buggy, hunt for fossils, jetboat or just get another Kiwi first under our collective belts.

# SAMUEL PARNELL

*First to give chippies—and the rest of the world—an eight-hour day*

London life in the 1830s was pretty tough. Many carpenters had to work 12–14 hour days in poor working conditions with not much pay, so it was no wonder that Samuel Duncan Parnell, a carpenter and joiner by trade, looked to New Zealand for a better lifestyle. He saved to pay the £126 for an intermediate passage to New Zealand for himself and his new wife, and the right to select 100 acres of country land and one town acre in the new Port Nicholson (Wellington) settlement.

Arriving in Petone on a New Zealand Company ship on 8 February 1840, Parnell found a town that was in need of his skills. One of Parnell's fellow ship passengers, George Hunter, who he'd become friendly with, approached Parnell to help him build a general store.

In a response that is worthy of a Hollywood movie script, Parnell said:

> I will do my best, but I must make this condition, Mr. Hunter, that on the job the hours shall only be eight for the day . . . There are twenty-four hours per day given us; eight of these should be for work, eight for sleep, and the remaining eight for recreation and in which for men to do what little things they want for themselves. I am ready to start to-morrow morning at eight o'clock, but it must be on these terms or none at all.

Hunter must've seen this coming: 'You know Mr. Parnell, that in London the bell rang at six o'clock, and if a man was not there ready to turn to he lost a quarter of a day.'

'We're not in London,' replied Parnell as he turned away.

George Hunter, realising that there was a shortage of skilled labour in the new colony, called him back and reluctantly agreed to Parnell's terms.

Aware that other labourers new to the country may accept 12-hour work days, and would therefore do him out of a job, Parnell saw that he had an opportunity to make a difference. He met with the workers and labourers disembarking from the ships and gained their support, creating a bit of a revolution in the process.

In October 1840, a meeting of workers, held on Lambton Quay, put forward the motion to work eight hours a day, from 8 a.m. to 5 p.m., and anyone not participating would be ducked into the harbour.

Employers were none too pleased, and the final frontier was the road built along the harbour towards the Hutt Valley, when labourers downed tools until an eight-hour day was agreed to.

Samuel Parnell (left) and the Eight-hour Day Committee wanted more sunshine and spare time; it's one committee that workers were thankful for

Parnell made his new life as a farmer, but also did many carpentry jobs, including the building of Homewood, now the UK high commissioner's residence on Hill Street, Thorndon.

In 1890, to mark 50 years of paid work which had helped establish the colony, the trade unions looked to the past and Parnell's place in history was remembered; he was identified as 'one who has done more for [the nation] than any, or all, the Acts of Parliament ever has, or could do'.

While the eight-hour working day was by then standard for tradesmen and labourers, other worker's groups, such as domestic servants, farmhands, shop assistants and clerks, all worked longer hours. In order to promote change, trade unions campaigned for universal shorter hours with annual processions in what became known as Eight-Hour Demonstration Day or Labour Day.

On 28 October 1890, Samuel Parnell was seated in a horse-drawn carriage at the head of the first annual Labour Day demonstration and was presented with an illuminated address that honoured him as 'the father of the eight hours movement'. Speaking at the Labour Day parade, he had stated that he was happy because an idea that had started in Petone was 'vibrating round the world'.

Parnell fell ill just a few weeks later and died. The city decided to give Parnell a public funeral and, on 20 December 1890, relays of men carried Parnell's coffin from Cambridge Terrace through the streets, where thousands had gathered, to the Wellington public cemetery—something that would be unlikely to happen to, say, a politician of today.

New Zealand legislated Labour Day to become a public holiday in 1899, and the first Labour Day that everyone got to celebrate was in 1900.

But it was not until the 1940s that the first Labour Government introduced the eight-hour day and 40-hour week as standard conditions for most workers—the first country to do so.

In 1962 the New Zealand Carpenters Union repaired Parnell's grave and provided a new headstone; Wellingtonians can visit it in the Bolton Street graveyard when they knock off their eight-hour working day.

The eight-hour day is now universally acknowledged and is practised in much of the Western world—in theory at least.

When planting out their potatoes and tomatoes, a task traditionally done on Labour Day to ensure fresh produce on the Christmas table, New Zealanders should give a thought to Samuel Parnell who championed the use of leisure time to feed the soul and the family.

## FIRST REFEREE'S WHISTLE

Before William Atack had the idea that etched him into history books, there must have been many exhausted referees with sore throats after yelling for an hour and a half at a bunch of fast-moving people lumbering around a paddock.

In June 1884, Atack—a 27-year-old sports journalist—weary from having to shout his directions and judgements to the Canterbury men in the rugby match he was reffing thought that there must be a better way of communicating. In his pocket he found a dog whistle, and as he fingered the whistle a brilliantly simple yet effective idea occurred to him. At the next match that he refereed, he suggested to the two teams that they play to the whistle; it was a world first, and now we barely even think about the peeping and shrill that punctuates our Saturday morning gatherings on netball courts and football fields around the nation.

Incidentally, the directness of William Atack's 'first' was echoed in his professional life; he was the general manager of the United Press Association (later to become the New Zealand Press Association) for an impressive 44 years. He was a precise and demanding character, and a well-respected journalist. A legend in his own lifetime, Atack was also accomplished on the rugby field, on the cricket pitch and on the sidelines of both games.

In 1930, at the age of 74, he called time on his career at the NZPA, and died sixteen years later, having changed the sound of sports worldwide. (See Cyril Brownlie page 76 for another significant whistle-stop moment in New Zealand history.)

# ACKNOWLEDGEMENTS

Much thanks and appreciation to everyone behind Te Ara online Encyclopedia and New Zealand History net—the amount of historical reference and knowledge available is truly outstanding. Thanks to the Ministries who invested in these resources and who put the time and effort into making these stories of our past so available. Thanks to the Alexander Turnbell Library and NASA for the photographs.

My sincere thanks to my commissioning editor, Nicola McCloy, for giving me this opportunity to learn so much more about Aotearoa/ New Zealand. Thanks to Siobhán Cantrill for her patience, and to Rebecca Lal for her keen eye and bright-minded editorial work. My heartfelt gratitude to Katie, Kendyl and Amy for putting up with—and sometimes feeding—'the writer in the corner', many thanks to Emma for cakes and tea, and to P-Dizzle for coffees. Thanks to JB for Bugger-all, thanks to Phil for clarifying early military arrivals. Aroha to Brendan Michael Kennedy for being so enthusiastic and very helpful in finding the leads to the historic law cases. Esteemed thanks to my uncle Greg for alerting me to the dog trials and the paper mills. Thanks to Craig Dylke whose dinosaur images are fantastic, but unfortunately couldn't find a home in this book. Many cheers to Pari, my first reader, for his enthusiastic encouragement when I needed it. Thanks to my team at JTM for understanding and supporting my need to be part-time, and thanks especially to Adam and Lynn for putting up with my random 'first' facts. Thanks to map-guru Charlotte Dawson for going the distance. Thanks to all who suggested firsts and offered words of encouragement. As always, my love and gratitude goes to my family, friends and whanau for . . . everything.

# BIBLIOGRAPHY


*The First Book of New Zealand Lists*, Compiled by Dale Williams, 1983

*The Dunmore Book of New Zealand Records*, The Dunmore Press Ltd, 1977

Keith Tonkin, *Four Great New Zealand Inventors*, Gilt Edge Publishing, 2003

Stephen Barnett, *The Book of New Zealand Records and Firsts*, Scholastic, 2011

John Bridges and David Downs, *No8 Wire: The Best of Kiwi Ingenuity*, Hodder Moa Beckett, 2000

Christine Cole Catley, *Bright Star: Beatrice Hill Tinsley, astronomer*, Cape Catley Ltd, 2006

Joan Druett, *She Captains, Heroines and Hellions of the Sea*, Simon & Schuster, 2000

Susanne and John Hill, *Richard Henry of Resolution Island*, John McIndoe, 1987

Keith Jackson and Alan McRobie, *Historical Dictionary of New Zealand*, Addison Wesley Longman New Zealand Limited, 1996

Wendy McGuinness & Miriam White, *Nation dates: significant events that have shaped the nation of New Zealand*, The Sustainable Future Institute, 2011

Veronika Meduna & Rebecca Priestly, *Atoms, Dinosaurs & DNA, 68 Great New Zealand Scientists*, Random House, 2008

Gordon Ogilvie, *The Riddle of Richard Pearse: The story of New Zealand's pioneer aviator and inventor*, Reed Books, 2003

Allan Sutherland, *New Zealand Famous Firsts and Related Records*, Universal Printers, 1960

http://www.nzhistory.net.nz/

http://www.teara.govt.nz/

http://www.nzedge.com/heroes/index.html

# INDEX OF NAMES